Data Visualization Techniques

TRENDS IN SOFTWARE

User Interface Software
ed. Len Bass and Prasun Dewan

Configuration Management
ed. Walter Tichy

Software Fault Tolerance
ed. Michael Lyu

Software Process
ed. Alfonso Fuggetta and Alexander Wolfe

Formal Methods for Real-Time Computing
ed. Constance Heitmeyer and Dino Mandrioli

Data Visualization Techniques
ed. Chandrajit Bajaj

Computer Supported Co-operative Work
ed. Michel Beaudouin-Lafon

Data Visualization Techniques

Edited by
Chandrajit Bajaj
University of Texas in Austin, USA

JOHN WILEY & SONS, LTD
Chichester · New York · Weinheim · Brisbane · Singapore · Toronto

Other Wiley Editorial Offices

John Wiley & Sons, Inc., 605 Third Avenue,
New York, NY 10158-0012, USA

Wiley-VCH Verlag, GmbH
Pappelallee 3, D-69469 Weinheim, Germany

Jacaranda Wiley Ltd, 33 Park Road, Milton,
Queensland 4064, Australia

John Wiley & Sons (Canada) Ltd, 22 Worcester Road,
Rexdale, Ontario M9W 1L1, Canada

John Wiley & Sons (Asia) Pte Ltd, 2 Clementi Loop #02-01,
Jin Xing Distripark, Singapore 129809

TA
1634
D373
1999

British Library Cataloguing in Publication Data

A catalogue record for this book is available from the British Library

ISBN 0 471 96356 9

Produced from files supplied by the authors and processed by Alden Bookset
Printed and bound in Great Britain by Biddles Ltd, Guildford and King's Lynn
This book is printed on acid-free paper responsibly manufactured from sustainable forestry in which at least two trees are planted for each one used for paper production

Contents

Series Editor's Preface

During 1990, the twentieth anniversary of *Software Practice and Experience*, two special issues (one on UNIX Tools and the other on the X Window System) were published. Each issue contained a set of refereed papers related to a single topic; the issues appeared a short time (roughly nine months) after the authors were invited to submit them. The positive experience with the special issues resulted in *Trends in Software*, a fast turn-around serial that devotes each issue to a specific topic in the software field. As with the special issues of SPE, each issue of *Trends* will be edited by an authority in the area.

By collecting together a comprehensive set of papers on a single topic, *Trends* makes it easy for readers to find a definitive overview of a given topic. By insuring timely publication, *Trends* guarantees readers that the information presented captures the state of the art. The collection of papers will be of practical value to software designers, researchers, practitioners and users in that field.

Papers in each issue of *Trends* are solicited by a guest editor who is responsible for soliciting them and ensuring that the selected papers span the topic. The guest editor then subjects each paper to the rigorous peer review expected in any archival journal. As much as possible, electronic communication (e.g. electronic mail) is used as the primary means of communication between the series editor, members of the editorial board, guest editor, authors, and referees. A style document and macro package is available to reduce the turn-around time by enabling authors to submit papers in camera-ready form. Papers are exchanged electronically in an immediately printable format.

Trends will appear roughly twice a year. We now have issues in interactive data visualization techniques and (shortly) computer supported co-operative work. Topics to be covered in forthcoming issues include other novel aspects of software.

The editorial board encourages readers to submit suggestions and comments. You may send them via electronic mail to **bala@research.att.com** or by postal mail to the address given below.

I would like to thank the editorial board as well as the staff at John Wiley for their help in making each issue of *Trends* a reality.

Balachander Krishnamurthy
Room D-229
AT&T Labs–Research
180 Park Avenue
Florham Park, NJ 07932
USA

Preface

Data visualization concerns the manipulation of sampled and computed data for comprehensive display. The goal of visualization is to bring to the user a deeper understanding of the data as well as the underlying physical laws and properties. Such visualization may be used to enlighten a physicist on the complex interaction between electrons, to guide the medical practitioner in a surgery situation, or simply to view the surface of a planet which has never been seen by human eyes.

Through the presentation of massive amounts of data as images, we allow the visualization user to rapidly prune useless information, focus on necessary information, and comprehend the science behind the data. Interaction with data brings another level of understanding. Static images can be misleading and can mask important features of the data. Motion in visualization brings out hidden features which are inherently dynamic. Interactive manipulation and control of visualization is an important tool which allows scientists to focus more quickly on the region of interest. In environments which are immersive, the motion is critical, to the point that delays or inconsistencies can make the viewer ill. In this case there is a desire to bound response time using time-critical techniques.

The important aspects of interactive visualization can be broken down into three categories:

Computation – the ability to compute a visualization speedily. This may include computing a polygonal approximation to an isosurface of a scalar function, or the computation of a particle trace through a time-dependent vector field, or any action which requires extracting an abstract object or representation from the data being examined.

Display – the ability to display the computed visualization quickly. Display encompasses both computed visualizations as listed above, as well as direct display methods such as volume visualization and ray tracing.

Querying – the ability to probe a displayed visualization interactively for the purpose of further understanding on a fine scale what is being displayed on a coarser scale.

In this book we propose to address the important aspects of interactivity in the visualization of scalar, vector and tensor field data. In addition, the book shall address data structures and algorithmic techniques for efficient computation and visualization in the time domain.

Chandrajit Bajaj
University of Texas at Austin, USA

List of Authors

Chandrajit L. Bajaj
TICAM TAY 2.400
University of Texas at Austin
Austin, TX 788712
USA
bajaj@ticam.utexas.edu

Barry Becker
Lawrence Livermore National Lab
PO Box 808 L-561
Livermore, CA 94550
USA
bob@igpp.llnl.gov

Roger Crawfis
Computer & Information SC
Ohio State University
395 Dreese Laboratories
2015 Neil Ave.
Columbus, OH 43210
USA
crawfis@cis.ohio-state.edu

Stefanie Hahmann
Laboratoire LMC-IMAG
Tour IRMA
BP 53
F-38041 GRENOBLE
Cedex 9
FRANCE
hahmann@imag.fr

David H. Laidlaw
California Institute of Technology
Caltech 139-74

Pasadena, CA 91125
USA
dhl@druggist.gg.caltech.edu

Nelson Max
Lawrence Livermore National Lab
PO Box 808 L-561
Livermore, CA 94550
USA
max2@llnl.gov

Valerio Pascucci
TICAM TAY 2.400
University of Texas at Austin
Austin, TX 788712
USA
pascucci@ticam.utexas.edu

Daniel R. Schikore
Center for Applied Scientific
Computing
Lawrence Livermore National Lab
PO Box 808 L-561
Livermore, CA 94550
USA
schikore@llnl.gov

Roni Yagel
Computer & Information SC
Ohio State University
395 Dreese Laboratories
2015 Neil Ave.
Columbus, OH 43210
USA
ryagel@magnus.ohio-state.edu

1

Visualization Paradigms

Chandrajit L. Bajaj

University of Texas, Austin

ABSTRACT

A wide variety of techniques have been developed for the visualization of scalar, vector and tensor field data. They range from volume visualization, to isocontouring, from vector field streamlines or scalar, vector and tensor topology, to functions on surfaces. This multiplicity of approaches responds to the requirements emerging from an even wider range of application areas such as computational fluid dynamics, chemical transport, fracture mechanics, new material development, electromagnetic scattering/absorption, neurosurgery, orthopedics, and drug design. In this chapter I present a brief overview of the visualization paradigms currently used in several of the above application areas. A major objective is to provide a roadmap that encompasses the majority of the currently available methods to allow each potential user/developer to select the techniques suitable for his/her purpose.

1.1 INTRODUCTION

Typically, informative visualizations are based on the combined use of multiple techniques. For example Figure 1.1 (Plate 1) shows the combined use of isocontouring, volume rendering and slicing to highlight and compare the internal 3D structure of three different vorticity fields. For a detailed description of each of the approaches I make reference to subsequent chapters in this book and previously published technical papers and books [Bow95, Cle93, HU94, KK93, NHM97, REE+94, Wat92].

1.2 VOLUME RENDERING

Volume rendering is a projection technique that produces image displays of three-dimensional volumetric data (see Figure 1.2 (Plate 2)). Its main characteristic is the

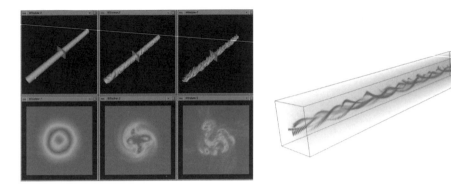

Figure 1.1 The combined display of isocontours, slicing and volume rendering used to highlight the 3D structure of vorticity fields. (See also color Plate 1)

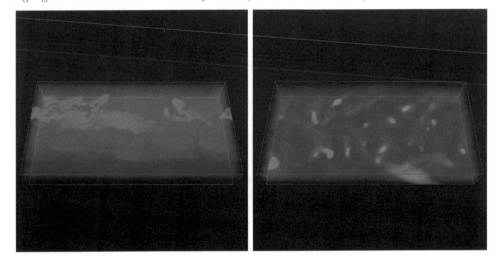

Figure 1.2 Two volume renderings showing snapshots of wind speed in a global climate model. (See also color Plate 2)

production of view-dependent snapshots of volumetric data, rather than the extraction of geometric information such as isocontouring.

Chapter 2 surveys alternate volume rendering algorithms reported in the literature. The two main classes of approach that have been developed differ mainly in the order of projection of the volume cells. Secondary distinctions arise from the differences in color accumulation and composition techniques to produce the final image.

Forward projection techniques traverse the volume (object space approach) projecting and display each volumetric cell or voxel. This approach takes advantage of graphics hardware acceleration by selecting appropriate drawing primitives to approximate the voxel image.

Backward projection techniques traverse the image (image space approach) and cast through the data volume, one light ray per pixel, accumulating color intensities along the ray to determine the final pixel color.

Cell projection and splatting are both forward projection techniques. In cell projection, the cells of the data volume are traversed and their images computed by subdivision into a polygonal approximation. In splatting, the samples of the volume are traversed and their contribution to the final image is computed by convolution with a reconstruction kernel. Cell projection techniques can be optimized by taking advantage of the spatial coherence of the volume cells both in the case of regular grids and in the case of unstructured meshes. Splatting has been shown to be a fast technique for hardware assisted scalar volume visualization, and has been extended to vector fields (see details in Chapter 5). Additional splatting techniques are developed for texture based visualization of velocity fields in the vicinity of contour surfaces (see details in Chapter 6).

Backward projection methods are accelerated by exploiting the coherence between adjacent rays. This idea has been implemented in a number of approaches using: (i) adaptive sampling along the rays depending on the "importance" of different regions (ii) templating the paths of parallel rays through regular grids, (iii) bounding with simple polyhedra significant regions that give the main contribution to the output image, or (iv) maintaining the front of propagating rays through irregular grids. The high computational cost of volume rendering in the spatial domain can sometimes be replaced by an asymptotically faster computation in the frequency domain [Lev92, Mal93, TL93].

1.3   ISOCONTOURING

Isocontouring is the extraction of constant valued curves and surfaces from 2D and 3D scalar fields. Interactive display and quantitative interrogation of isocontours helps in determining the overall structure of a scalar field (see Figure 1.3) and its evolution over time (see Figure 1.4 (Plate 3)).

Chapter 3 surveys the most commonly used isocontouring algorithms along with recent improvements that permit rapid evaluation of multiple isocontour queries, in an interactive environment. Traditional isocontouring techniques examine each cell of a mesh to test for intersection with the isocontour of interest. Accelerated isocontouring can be achieved by preprocessing the input scalar field both in its domain (the geometry of the input mesh) and in its range (the values of the sampled scalar field).

On the one hand, one takes advantage of the known adjacency information of mesh cells (domain space optimization). Given a single cell c on an isocontour component one can trace the entire isocontour component from c, by propagating from cell to cell using inter-cell adjacency. This reduces the search for isocontour components from a search in the entire input mesh to a search in a much smaller subset called the *seed set*. A *seed set* is a subset of the mesh cells which has at least one cell on each connected component of each isocontour. From this typically very small seed set of mesh cells one searches for starting cells for each component of the desired isocontour and then applies contour propagation through cell adjacencies.

On the other hand, one independently optimizes the search for isocontours, exploiting the simplicity of the range of the scalar field (range space optimization). The values of the field are scalars that in range space form an interval. Within each cell of the mesh (or of mesh cells of the seed set) the scalar field usually has a small continuous variation that can be represented in range space as a (small) subinterval. The isocontour computation is hence reduced in range space to the search for all the segments that intersect the currently selected isovalue w. This search can be optimally performed using well known interval tree or segment tree data structures.

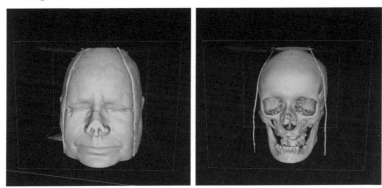

Figure 1.3 Skin and bone head models extracted as two different isocontours from the same volumetric MRI data of the Visible Human female.

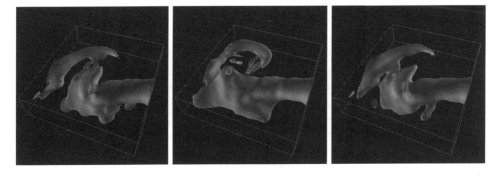

Figure 1.4 Three isocontours of wind speed that show the time evolution of air dynamics in a global climate model. (See also color Plate 3)

1.4 FLOW VISUALIZATION

Visualization of vector fields is generally more complicated than visualizing scalar fields due to the increased amount of information inherent in vector data. Clearly vector data can be contracted to scalar quantities, for example by computation of vector magnitude, scalar product with a given vector, or magnitude of vorticity. In this case, scalar visualization techniques such as isosurfaces and volume rendering can be applied. Additional approaches to visualization of vector fields include iconography, particle tracking, and qualitative global flow visualization techniques. Chapter 5 reviews flow visualization techniques while Chapter 6 describes more in detail the approaches designed to take advantage of currently existing graphics hardware to increase performance. For additional detail, refer to the papers cited in these two chapters.

Particle tracking or advection techniques are based on following the trajectory of a theoretically massless particle in a flow. In its simplest form, the path traversed by a particle in a steady flow is called a *streamline*. If the flow is unsteady, or time-varying, the path followed by a particle over time is called a *path line*. A curve resulting from a number of particles emitted at regular or irregular intervals from a single source is called a *streak line*. Numerical techniques commonly used for evaluating the above equation include Euler and Runge-Kutta methods. In the case of incompressible flow, a single stream-function in 2D can be constructed so that the contours of the stream-function are streamlines of the vector field. In 3D, a pair of dual stream functions is required, and streamlines will occur as the intersections of isocontours of the two functions [KM92].

Particle tracking techniques may also be extended by grouping multiple particles together to form a *stream ribbon, stream surface, stream tube* or *flow volume*. Global techniques such as Line Integral Convolution present a qualitative view of the vector field which presents intuitively meaningful visualizations for the user. Flow "probes" may be placed at user-specified or computed locations to reveal local properties of the flow field such as direction, speed, divergence, vorticity, etc. Properties are mapped to a geometric representation called an *icon*. The complexity of the icon increases with the amount of information that it is designed to represent. Representing curl (vorticity), which is itself a vector field with additional physical meaning, can be achieved by a cylindrical icon with candy-striping to indicate both the direction and magnitude of vorticity.

1.5   QUANTIFICATION

In the quest for interrogative visualization [Baj88], in which the user can not only see the data, but navigate and query for increased understanding, the ability to quantify and perform volumetric measurements is vital. Another challenge to visualization is to give quantitative information concerning time-dependent studies and time-varying structures (e.g. flow). In the study of paralysis, researchers are constructing models of spinal cords and regions of damaged cord from histological samples. Figure 1.5 (Plate 4) (left) is an example of a histological slice of an injured rat spine. In Figure 1.5 (Plate 4) (right), the damaged region has been reconstructed as a surface, and is visualized along with orthogonal slices of the 3D histological specimen. Traditionally, spinal damage has been modeled as an expanding cylindrical region. The ability to define the region of damage and measure the surface area and volume of the region more accurately are promising tools in developing a greater understanding of cysts and how they develop.

Chapter 7 reviews tissue classification techniques using local reconstructions of band limited samplings, and Bayesian statistics. Such classification provides the means to accurately identify (for isocontouring and volume rendering) and quantify the relevant substructures of three-dimensional images.

Chapter 4 reviews the shape analysis and visualization of free form surface models used in computer aided geometric design and computer graphics. The analysis tools prove essential to detecting surface imperfections as well as higher-order inter-

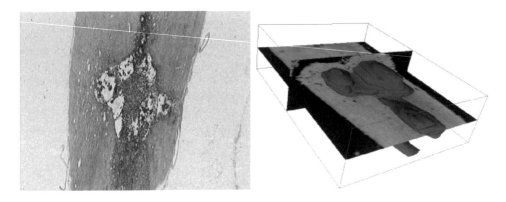

Figure 1.5 (Left) Histological sample of a rat spine. (Right) Reconstruced spinal lesion within slices of 3D histological volume. (See also color Plate 4)

patch smoothness. Related research on free-form surfaces visualization are addressed in [BR94, BBB+97].

Three special cases of volumetric quantification which are prevalent in data visualization applications apply to the following data types:

- **Contours** – surfaces which are created through isocontouring of scalar data
- **Slices** – surfaces which are formed by tiling multiple planar cross-sections of objects
- **Union of balls** – also known as the solvent accessible surface and common in molecular visualization

1.5.1   Contour Quantification

Bajaj, Pascucci and Schikore [BPS97a] introduce the systematic quantification of metric properties of volumetric data and the relative isocontours. Given an isovalue w one can compute the surface area of the corresponding isosurface, the volume of the *inside region* or any other metric property (also called signature) function of w. The plot of the signatures gives rise to an interface that drives the user in the direct selection of *interesting* isovalues. Figure 1.6 (Plate 5) shows the direct selection of noiseless isosurfaces corresponding to skin and bone tissues which correspond to the maxima of the gradient-weighted area signature.

1.5.2   Sliced Data

Objects are frequently reconstructed from serial sections [BCL96a, BCL96b]. In this case, volume properties can be accurately computed using the following equation for prismatoids, a triangular tiling of two parallel contours: $V = \frac{h}{6}(B_1 + 4M + B_2)$ where B_1 is the area of lower base, B_2 is the area of upper base, M is the area of the midsection joining the bases, and h is the separation between the contours. With n parallel slices of contours equally spaced, the composite volume computation results in:

$$V' = \frac{h}{6}(B_1 + 4\sum_{1}^{n-1} M_i + 2\sum_{2}^{n-1} B_i + B_n).$$

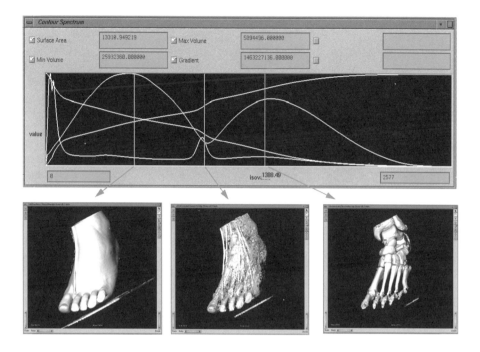

Figure 1.6   Three isosurfaces of the same volumetric MRI scan. The vertical bars in the spectrum interface (top) mark the selected isovalues. (See also color Plate 5)

1.5.3   Union of Balls

The geometric, combinatorial and quantitative structure of the union of a set of balls has been presented by Edelsbrunner and Delfindao [Ede95, DE95]. The union of balls model is equivalent to the space filling model used to represent molecules, where each atom is approximated by a ball with a relative van der Waals radius. Deeper insight into the properties of a molecule in solution is provided by the computation of the solvent accessible surface and the solvent excluded surface [SSO96]. The two surfaces are defined by idealizing the solvent molecule (e.g. water) as a single ball and computing the boundary of the region that can be accessed by the solvent center (solvent accessible offset of the union of balls model of the molecule) or the boundary of the region that cannot be reached by any point of the solvent (solvent excluded). On the basis of the union of balls model exact representations of both the surfaces can be computed efficiently [BLMP97] (see Figure 1.7 (Plate 6)).

1.6   DATA REDUCTION

Mesh reduction or simplification refers to a broad category of techniques designed to trade space and complexity for accuracy in representation of a surface or volume

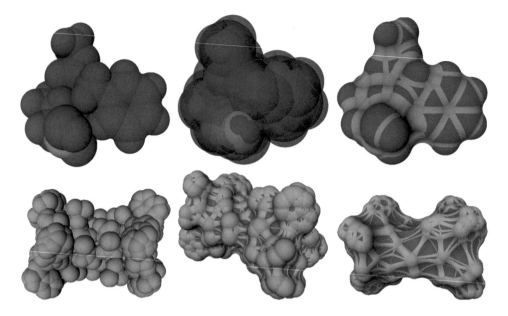

Figure 1.7 (Top) Union of balls, solvent accessible and solvent excluded surfaces of the Nutrasweet molecule with respect to the same solvent. (Bottom) Solvent excluded surface of the Gramicidin molecule with respect to three increasing solvent radii. (See also color Plate 6)

mesh. Like isocontouring, mesh reduction is an algorithmic approach used to prepro-cess the input dataset to make it more suitable for display or analysis queries. The difference is that while isocontouring extracts an *interesting* feature like a particular isosurface from a volumetric dataset, mesh reduction is meant to generate a reduced version of the volume itself to speed up postprocessing. Figure 1.8 (Plate 7) demon-strates mesh reduction applied to 2D functional data, in this case a slice of MRI data. Related results come from several research communities, including Geographi-cal Information Systems (GIS), Computational Fluid Dynamics (CFD), and Virtual

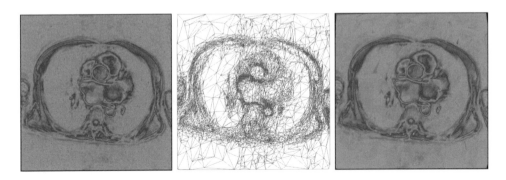

Figure 1.8 Original data (left), reduced triangulation (center), reduced image (right). (See also color Plate 7)

Environments/Virtual Reality (VE/VR). Each community has much the same goal for achieving interactivity with very large sets of data. An initial classification of techniques can be made by distinguishing between *static simplification*, in which a single resolution output is computed from a high-resolution input based on given simplification criteria, and *dynamic simplification*, in which hierarchical triangulations are computed, from which reduced triangulations can be rapidly extracted depending on time dependent metrics such as distance from the viewer, location in the field of view, and approximation error tolerance.

Height-field reduction: A driving application for reduction of height-fields is GIS. A wide range of techniques are based on extraction of key points or edges from the originally dense set of points, followed by a constrained Delaunay triangulation [DFP85, FFNP84, FL79, PDDT94, Tsa93, WJ92]. Silva, et al. [SMK95] use a greedy method for inserting points into an initially sparse mesh, reporting both better and faster reduction compared to a freely available terrain reduction tool. A survey by Lee [Lee91] reviews methods for computing reduced meshes by both point insertion and point deletion. Bajaj and Schikore [BS95, BS96a] developed practical techniques for measuring the local errors introduced by simplification operations and bound the global error accumulated by multiple applications. Their techniques begin with simple scalar fields and extend easily to multi-valued fields, and those defined on arbitrary surfaces. Geometric error in the surface as well as functional error in the data are bounded in a uniform manner. Topology preserving, error-bounded mesh simplification has also been explored [BS97]. Figure 1.9 (Plate 8) demonstrates geometric mesh reduction while Figure 1.8 (Plate 7) demonstrates mesh reduction applied to 2D functional data.

Figure 1.9 Three snapshots of geometric mesh simplification of an engine block. (See also color Plate 8)

Geometry reduction: Geometric mesh reduction has been approached from several directions. In the reduction of polygonal models, Turk [Tur92] uses point repulsion on the surface of a polygonal model to generate a set of vertices for retriangulation. Schroeder, et al. [SZL92] decimate dense polygonal meshes, generated by Marching Cubes [LC87], by deletion of vertices based on an error criteria, followed by local retriangulation with the goal of maintaining a good aspect ratio in the resulting triangulation. Errors incurred from local retriangulation are not propagated to the simplified mesh, hence there is no global error control. Rossignac, et al. [RB93] use clustering and merging of features of an object which are geometrically close, but may not be topologically connected. In this scheme, long thin objects may collapse to an edge and small objects may contract to a point. Hamann [Ham94] applies a similar technique in which triangles are considered for deletion based on curvature estimates at the vertices. Reduction may be driven by mesh resolution or, in the case of functional surfaces, root-mean-square error. He, et al. [HHK+95] perform mesh reduction by volume sampling and low-pass filtering an object. A multi-resolution triangle mesh is extracted from the resulting multi-resolution volume buffer using traditional isosurfacing techniques. Hoppe, et al. [HDD+93] perform time-intensive mesh optimization based on the definition of an energy function which balances the need for accurate geometry with the desire for compactness in representation. The level of mesh simplification is controlled by parameters in the energy function which penalize meshes with large numbers of vertices, as well as a spring constant which helps guide the energy minimization to a desirable result.

In [Hop96], Hoppe introduces *Progressive Meshes*, created by applying optimization with the set of basic operations reduced to only an *edge contraction*. Scalar attributes are handled by incorporating them into the energy function. Ronfard, et al. [RR96] also apply successive edge contraction operations to compute a wide range of levels-of-detail for triangulated polyhedra. Edges are extracted from a priority queue based on a computed *edge cost* such that edges of lesser significance are removed first. Cohen, et al. [CVM+96] introduce *Simplification Envelopes* to guide mesh simplification with global error bounds. Envelopes are an extension of *offset surfaces* which serve as an extreme boundary for the desired simplified surface. Lindstrom, et al. [LKR+96] impose a recursive triangulation on a regular terrain and compute preprocessing metrics at various levels of resolution, which permits real-time adaptive triangulation for interactive fly-through. Funkhouser, et al. [FS93] describe adaptive display algorithms for rendering complex environments at a sustained frame rate using multiple levels of detail.

Delaunay techniques for static simplification have been extended to create hierarchies of Delaunay triangulations from which a simplified mesh can be extracted on the fly [dBD95]. Successive levels of the hierarchy are created by deleting points from the current level and retriangulating according to the Delaunay criteria, giving the hierarchical structure of a *directed acyclic graph* (DAG). Puppo [Pup96] improves on the approach of de Berg by augmenting the DAG with information on which triangles between successive resolutions are overlapping. With this information, the problem of extracting a triangulation from the DAG is simplified and requires no backtracking. It is shown that for a given triangulation criteria, the optimal triangulation satisfying the criteria which is embedded in the DAG can be extracted in optimal time. Cohen and Levanoni [COL96] adopt a tree representation for hierarchical Delaunay triangulation and demonstrate techniques for maintaining temporal coherence between successive triangulations. The technique is demonstrated for relatively sparse terrains, and it remains to be seen whether the constraints imposed by a tree representation will restrict simplification for dense triangulated terrains.

Wavelets [Mal89, Dau92] have been utilized for their multi-resolution applications in many areas of computer graphics and visualization [SDS96], including image compression [DJL92a], surface description [DJL92b, EDD+95, CPD+96], tiling of con-

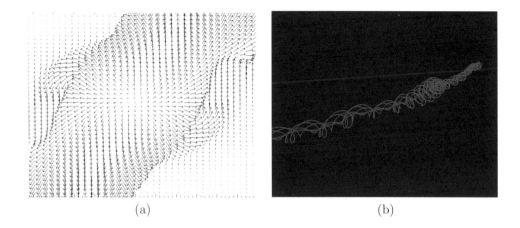

(a)   (b)

Figure 1.10   (a) Arrow plot of a two-dimensional vector field; (b) streamline along focus in the vortex core surrounded by nearby streamlines. (See also color Plate 9)

tours [Mey94] and curve and surface editing [FS94, ZSS97]. A number of multi-resolution volume hierarchies have been proposed for developing adaptive volume rendering and isocontouring [Mur92, Mur95, CDM+94, WV94].

1.7   TOPOLOGY

Field topology refers to the analysis and classification of critical points and computation of relationships between the critical points of field data [Del94]. Computation and display of field topology can provide a compact global view of what is otherwise a very large set of data. Techniques such as volume rendering and line integral convolution provide qualitative global views of field topology.

Vector Topology: Given a continuous vector field, the locations at which the vector becomes zero are called critical points. Analysis of the critical points can determine behavior of the vector field in the local region. In a 2D vector field, critical points are classified into *sources*, *sinks*, and *saddles* (see Figure 1.11(a)), with both spiral and non-spiral cases for sources and sinks [HH90, HH89, GLL91]. In 3D, additional critical points include the *spiral-saddle* [HH90], which is useful for locating vortex cores, as shown in Figure 1.10 (Plate 9).

Scalar Topology: Scalar field topology can be viewed as a special case of vector field topology, where the vector field is given by the gradient of the scalar function [BS96b]. Critical points in a scalar field are defined by a zero gradient, and can be classified into *maxima*, *minima*, *saddle points*, and degenerate cases, as illustrated in Figure 1.11(b). Two examples are given in Figure 1.12 (Plate 10).

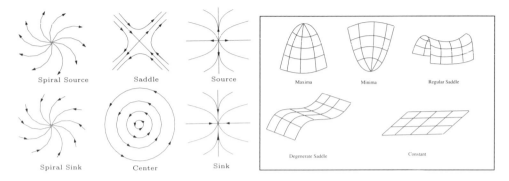

Figure 1.11   (a) Classification of vector field zeros; (b) critical point classification for scalar field.

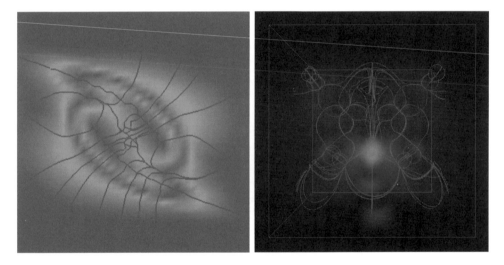

Figure 1.12   Two examples of scalar topology of 2D (left) and 3D (right) scalar fields. The 2D case shows the scalar topology displayed over a color-map of the density in a pion collision simulation. The 3D case is that of the scalar topology diagram of the wave function computed for a high-potential iron protein. (See also color Plate 10)

1.8   FUNCTIONS ON SURFACES

Functions on surfaces visualization deals with the visual display of scalar functions whose domain is restricted to an arbitrary geometric surface in three dimensions. The surface may be the isosurface of another scalar field, or simply a geometric domain with an associated function field [FLN+90, BOP92, BX94, BBX95].

Figure 1.13 Visualization of functions on surfaces. (Top-left) The electrostatic energy potential shown on an isosurface of van der Waals interaction potenial energy. (Top-right) Pressure distribution around the earth globe. (Bottom-left) Pressure distribution on the surface of a jet engine modeled and displayed using tensor product surface splines. (Bottom-right) Stress distribution on a human knee joint based on static loads. (See also color Plate 11)

2

Efficient Techniques for Volume Rendering of Scalar Fields

Roni Yagel

Department of Computer and Information Science, The Ohio State University

ABSTRACT

The task of efficient rendering of today's volumetric datasets is still being tackled by several research groups around the world. A quick calculation of the amount of computation required for interactive rendering of a high-resolution volume puts us in the teraflop range. Yet the demand to support such rendering capabilities is increasing due to emerging technologies such as virtual surgery simulation and rapid prototyping.

There are five main approaches to overcoming this seemingly insurmountable performance barrier: (i) data reduction by means of model extraction or data simplification, (ii) realization of special-purpose volume rendering engines, (iii) software-based algorithm optimization and acceleration, (iv) implementation on general purpose parallel architectures, and (v) use of contemporary off-the-shelf graphics hardware.

In this presentation we first describe the vision of real-time high-resolution volume rendering and estimate the computing power it demands. We survey the state of the art in rapid volume rendering and compare the achievements and effectivity of the various approaches. We look ahead and describe the remaining challenges and some possible ways of providing the needs of this ever demanding field.

2.1   INTRODUCTION

Traditional 3D graphics is based on surface representation. Most common are polygon-based surfaces for which affordable special-purpose rendering hardware has been

---

developed in the last decade. As an alternative representation for surfaces we have
been exploring volumes. Our screens are composed of a two-dimensional array (raster)
of pixels, each representing a unit of area. A volume is a three-dimensional array of
cubic elements, each representing a unit of space. In the same way that a screen can be
used to store two dimensional objects such as lines and digital pictures, a volume can
be used to store three-dimensional geometric objects and three-dimensional pictures.

The main disadvantage of volumes is their immense size. A medium-resolution volume of $256 \times 256 \times 256$ requires storage for 16 million voxels. These have to be
processed in order to generate an image of this 3D object onto a 2D screen. However,
volumes have some major advantages: they can represent the interior of objects, and
not only the outer shell as surfaces do. Rendering and processing does not depend on
the object's complexity or type, it depends only on volume resolution. It easily supports operations such as subtraction, addition, collision detection, and deformation.
For a complete comparison see [KCY93]. Although the computing power required for
volume rendering is immense, so are the benefits from some potential applications
which rely on such capability. One such application is the simulation of surgery on a
virtual patient [YSW+96]. The patient is first "digitized" by a medical scanner such
as CT, MRI, or Ultrasound. Surgery can then be planned, rehearsed, and redesigned
while operating on the digital model in a non-threatening virtual environment. It is
obvious that such a "medical flight simulator" must provide interactions and behaviors
that are similar enough to the "real world" in order to maximize transfer to actual
practice. We believe that real-time interaction is the most essential requirement and
that practitioners prefer to operate in an interactive environment even if it is rendered
in a somewhat less realistic way.

The simplest way to implement viewing is to traverse all the volume, regarding each
voxel as a 3D point that is transformed by the viewing matrix and then projected
onto a Z-buffer and drawn onto the screen. This approach is also called *object space
rendering or forward rendering.*

The back-to-front (BTF) algorithm is essentially the same as the Z-buffer method
with one exception that is based on the observation that the voxel array is presorted in
a fashion that allows scanning of its component in an order of decreasing or increasing
distance from the observer. Exploiting this presortedness of the voxel array, traversal
of the volume in the BTF algorithm is done in order of decreasing distance to the
observer. This avoids the need for a Z-buffer for hidden voxel removal considerations
by simply drawing the current voxel on top of previously drawn voxels ("painter's algorithm") or by compositing the current voxel with the screen value [FZY84, FGR85].

The front-to-back (FTB) algorithm is essentially the same as BTF only that now
the voxels are traversed in increasing distance order [RGC87]. It should be observed
that while in the basic Z-buffer method it is impossible to support the rendering of
semitransparent materials since voxels are mapped to the screen in arbitrary order.
Compositing is based on a computation that simulates the passage of light through
several materials. In this computation the order of materials is crucial. Therefore,
translucency can easily be realized in both BTF and FTB, in which objects are mapped
to the screen in the order in which the light traverses the scene.

One of the main difficulties in the naive approach described above is the proper
signal reconstruction and resampling required when one transforms a discrete set of
samples. One solution is based on transforming each slice from voxel space to pixel

space using 3D affine transformation (shearing) [Han90, LL94, SS91] followed by projection onto the screen in an FTB fashion, and blending with the projection formed by previous slices [DCH88].

Westover [Wes90] has introduced another reconstruction technique for forward viewing methods - the *splatting* algorithm. Each voxel, after being transformed into screen space, is blurred, based on a 2D lookup table (footprint) that spreads the voxel's energy across multiple pixels. These are then composited with the image array.

In contrast to the forward viewing approach, the *backward viewing* scheme (also called the *image space* method) casts a ray from the eye, through each pixel on the screen, into the volume data, until it intersects an opaque object or accumulates an opaque value through compositing [Lev88a, TT84, UK88]. Backward viewing is much more powerful than forward viewing since it can be extended to support global illumination and volume deformation. Global illumination is based on recursively following secondary rays and shadow feelers [YCK92], as in traditional ray tracing. Volume deformation is based on bending the path the rays take, according to the influence of "gravity fields" called *deflectors* [KY95].

The simplest method for implementing resampling performs zero-order interpolation to locate the nearest voxel while stepping along the discrete ray representation which is generated by a 3D line algorithm [SSW86]. Alternatively, the volume is sampled at the intersection points of the ray and the voxels' faces, its value is interpolated, and then composited [UK88]. A more precise algorithm uses higher-order interpolation to estimate the appropriate value at evenly spaced sample points along the ray [KH84], [Lev88a], [Sab88].

Since ray casting follows only primary rays, it does not directly support the simulation of light phenomena such as reflection, shadows, and refraction. As an alternative we have developed the 3D raster ray tracer (RRT) [YCK92] that recursively considers both primary and secondary rays and thus can create 'photorealistic' images. In conventional ray tracing algorithms, analytical rays, searching for the closest intersection, are intersected with the object list. In contrast, in our approach 3D discrete rays, searching for the first surface voxels, are traversed through the 3D raster. Encountering a nontransparent voxel represents a ray-surface hit.

How much computation is involved in rendering a volumetric dataset? To answer this question we need to divide the rendering task into two parts: illumination and viewing. *Illumination* determines the color ($RGB\alpha$) of a voxel, based on some classification functions, transfer functions, and illumination models. These can vary from a simple illumination model (threshold, followed by color lookup, and depth shading) to the most complex illumination (segmentation, followed by multivariate transfer function, followed by multi-scattering illumination model [Kru90, Max95]). In the following discussion we will assume that the volume has been illuminated already and we are left with the task of rendering the 3D grids of $RGB\alpha$ values.

Assume we need to render a volume of size $N \times N \times N$ voxels. Assume also that we employ a forward rendering approach and a splatting-based reconstruction. Therefore, each voxel has to go through transformation, followed by K^2 compositing steps (assuming the footprint size is K). For a BTF order, compositing is implemented by

$$A = \alpha + A \cdot (1 - \alpha)$$
$$C_\lambda = c_\lambda \cdot \alpha + C_\lambda \cdot (1 - \alpha) \tag{1}$$

where λ stands for the three color bands, RGB, C and A denote the color and opacity of the accumulation buffer, and c and α, that of the composited sample. Simple arithmetic will give us:

$$T = N^3 \cdot ((16t_m + 12t_a) + K^2 \cdot (3t_m + 8t_a)) \qquad (2)$$

Where t_a and t_m denote addition and multiplication time, respectively. For medium resolution and image quality ($N = 256$ and $K = 3$), we require approximately $1.8 \cdot 10^9$ floating point (FP) operations for rendering one frame, or $5.4 \cdot 10^{10}$ for real-time rendering (30 frames per second). If we try to render a higher resolution volume and better image quality ($N = 512$ and $K = 5$), we will require $4 \cdot 10^{10}$ FP per frame and $1.2 \cdot 10^{12}$ FP for real-time rendering. One can go through a similar exercise for the backward rendering approach, which will yield similar results.

It is obvious that one can not hope to have real-time volume rendering in the near future without investing time, effort, and ingenuity in accelerating the process through software optimizations and hardware implementations. This chapter surveys recent advances in this quest.

There are five main approaches to overcoming this seemingly insurmountable performance barrier: (i) data reduction by means of model extraction or data simplification, (ii) realization of special-purpose volume rendering engines, (iii) software-based algorithm optimization and acceleration, described in Section 2, (iv) implementation on general-purpose parallel architectures, described in Section 3, and (v) use of contemporary off-the-shelf graphics hardware, described in Section 4. In this chapter, we consider the last three, namely, software optimization, parallel implementation, and use of graphics hardware - methods which we consider to be the most prolific and successful. We conclude, in Section 5, by looking at the future of volume rendering acceleration.

2.2 ALGORITHM OPTIMIZATION

2.2.1 Optimizing Object Space Forward Rendering

Some methods have been suggested to reduce the amount of computation needed for the transformation by exploiting the spatial coherency between voxels. These methods are: recursive "divide and conquer" [Mea82], precalculated tables [FGR85], incremental transformation [MYS92], and shearing-based transforms [Han90].

The first method [Mea82] exploits coherency in voxel space by representing the 3D volume by an octree. A group of neighboring voxels having the same value (or similar, up to a threshold value) may, under some restrictions, be grouped into a uniform cubic subvolume. This aggregate of voxels can be transformed and rendered as a uniform unit instead of processing each of its voxels. In addition, since each octree node has eight equally sized octants, given the transformation of the parent node, the transformation of its sub-octants can be efficiently computed. The table-driven transformation method [FGR85] is based on the observation that volume transformation involves the multiplication of the matrix elements with integer values which are always in the range $[1, \ldots, N]$, where N is the volume resolution. Therefore, in a short preprocessing stage each matrix element t_{ij} is allocated a table $T_{ij}[N]$ such that $T_{ij}[k] = t_{ij} \cdot k$. During the transformation stage, coordinate by matrix multiplication is replaced by table lookup.

The incremental transformation method is based on the observation that the transformation of a voxel $[x+1, y, z]$ can be incrementally computed given the transformed vector $[x', y', z']$ of the voxel at $[x, y, z]$. To employ this approach, all volume elements, including the empty ones, have to be transformed. This approach is therefore more suitable to parallel architecture where it is desired to keep the computation pipeline busy [MYS92]. This approach is especially attractive for vector processors since the transformations of the set of voxels $[x + 1, 1, z], [x + 1, 2, z], \ldots, [x + 1, N, z]$, called *beam* and denoted by $[x + 1, 1 \ldots N, z]$, can be computed from the transformation of the vector $[x', (1 \ldots N)', z']$ by adding to each element in this vector the same three matrix elements.

The shearing algorithm decomposes the 3D affine transformation into five 1D shearing transformations [Han90]. The major advantage of this approach is its ability (using simple averaging techniques) to overcome some of the sampling problems causing the production of low-quality images. In addition, this approach replaces the 3D transformation by five 1D transformations which require only one floating-point addition each.

The splatting algorithm requires extensive filtering and is therefore very time-consuming. We have described [SCK+93] a simplified approximation to the splatting method for interactive volume viewing in which only voxels comprising the object's surface are maintained. This approach also provides a simple incremental refinement of image quality: when the volume is manipulated by the user, only one point per voxel is rendered, interactively producing a low-quality image. When the volume remains stationary and unchanged for some short period, the rendering system renders the rest of the points to increase image quality. These ideas were further explored to allow non-binary surfaces by extracting all voxels that contribute to the final image [YESK95].

Another efficient implementation of the splatting algorithm, called hierarchical splatting [LH91] uses a pyramid data structure to hold a multi-resolution representation of the volume. For a volume of N^3 resolution, the pyramid data structure consists of a sequence of $\log N$ volumes. The first volume contains the original dataset; the next volume in the sequence is half the resolution of the previous one. Each of its voxels contains an average of eight voxels in the higher resolution volume. According to the desired image quality, this algorithm scans the appropriate level of the pyramid in a BTF order. Each element is splatted using the appropriately sized splat. The splats themselves are approximated by polygons which can efficiently be rendered by graphics hardware (see Section 4).

It seems that in forward methods voxels need to be transformed and tested against the screen in order to avoid compositing at already opaque pixels. Reynolds, et al. [RGC87] developed the *dynamic screen* which decodes the screen lines as run-length of non-opaque pixels. The transformation guarantees that a row of voxels always transforms into a row of pixels. These can be tested against each other in runs rather than by comparing individual voxels. This idea was later adopted for expediting the shearing algorithm [LL94].

The shearing algorithm was also optimized [LL94] by devising a factorization that is faster than the original decomposition [Han90]. Also, a data structure was introduced for encoding spatial coherence in unclassified volumes (i.e. scalar fields with no precomputed opacity).

2.2.2   Optimizing Image Space Backward Rendering

Backward viewing of volumes, based on casting rays, has three major variations: parallel (orthographic) ray casting, perspective ray casting, and ray tracing. The first two are variations of ray casting, in which only primary rays, that is, rays from the eye through the screen, are followed. Ray casting can further be divided into methods that support only parallel viewing, that is, when the eye is at infinity and all rays are parallel to one viewing vector. This viewing scheme is used in applications that would not benefit from perspective distortion, such as biomedicine. Alternatively, ray casting can also be implemented to support perspective viewing. Since ray casting follows only primary rays, it does not directly support the simulation of light phenomena such as reflection, shadows, and refraction. As an alternative we have developed the 3D raster ray tracer (RRT) [YCK92] that recursively considers both primary and secondary rays and thus can create "photorealistic" images.

The examination of existing methods for speeding up the process of ray casting reveals that most of them rely on one or more of the following principles: (1) pixel space coherency (2) object space coherency (3) inter-ray coherency (4) frame coherency, and (5) space-leaping. We now turn to describe each of those in more detail.

Pixel space coherency

There is a high coherency between pixels in image space. That is, it is highly probable that between two pixels having identical or similar color we will find another pixel having the same (or similar) color. Therefore it is observed that it might be the case that we could avoid sending a ray for such obviously identical pixels.

The adaptive image supersampling exploits the pixel space coherency. It was originally developed for traditional ray tracing [BFGS86] and later adapted to volume rendering [Lev90b]. First, rays are cast from only a subset of the screen pixels (e.g., every other pixel). "Empty pixels" residing between pixels with similar value are assigned an interpolated value. In areas of high image gradient additional rays are cast to resolve ambiguities.

Object space coherency

The extension of the pixel space coherency to 3D states that there is coherency between voxels in object space. Therefore, it is observed that it should be possible to avoid sampling in 3D regions having uniform or similar values.

van Walsum, et al. [vWHVP91] have exploited voxel space coherency. In their method the ray starts sampling the volume at low frequency (i.e., large steps between sampling points). If a large value difference is encountered between two adjacent samples, additional samples are taken between them to resolve ambiguities in these high-frequency regions. Recently, this basic idea was extended to efficiently lower the sampling rate either in areas where only small contributions of opacities are made, or in regions where the volume is homogeneous [DH92]. This method efficiently detects regions of low presence or low variation by employing a pyramid of volumes that decode the minimum and maximum voxel value in a small neighborhood, as well as the distance between these measures.

Inter-ray coherency

There is a great deal of coherency between rays in parallel viewing, that is, all rays, although having different origin, have the same slope. Therefore, the steps these rays take when traversing the volume are similar. We exploit this coherency to avoid the computation involved in navigating the ray through voxel space. As shown in Figure 2.1, the ith sample along the ray lies in the same relative position within a cell. Therefore, part of the computation needed for trilinear interpolation can be performed in a preprocessing stage and stored in the template for later use at rendering time.

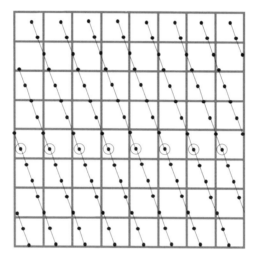

Figure 2.1   Template-driven traversal with sub-voxel addresses for object space supersampling. The seventh sample along each ray is circled.

The template-based method [YK92, Yag92] utilizes the inter-ray coherency. Observing that, in parallel viewing, all rays have the same form, it was realized that there is no need to reactivate the discrete line algorithm for each ray. Instead, we can compute the form of the ray once and store it in a data structure called a ray-template. All rays can then be generated by following the ray template. The rays, however, differ in the exact positioning of the appropriate portion of the template, an operation that has to be performed very carefully. For this purpose a plane that is parallel to one of the volume faces is chosen to serve as a base-plane for the template placement. The image is projected by sliding the template along that plane emitting a ray at each of its pixels. This placement guarantees a complete and uniform tessellation of the volume.

The template-based algorithm starts by finding the base-plane, the image extent, and a ray-template. The base-plane is that one of the three object space planes onto which the image is projected to the largest area. From this plane, and within the projected region of the volume, parallel rays are cast into the volume by repeating the sequence of steps specified by the ray-template. The result of the second phase of the algorithm is a projection of the volume on the base-plane. The third phase of the algorithm transforms the projected image from the base-plane to the screen-plane.

The regularity and simplicity of this efficient algorithm make it very attractive for hardware implementation [Yag91] and for massively parallel computers such as the CM-2 [SS92].

Frame coherency

When an animation sequence is generated, in many cases there is not much difference between successive images. Therefore, much of the work invested to produce one image may be used to expedite the generation of the next image.

Yagel and Shi [YS93] have reported on a method for speeding up the process of volume rendering a sequence of images. It is based on exploiting coherency between consecutive images to shorten the path rays take through the volume. This is achieved by providing each ray with the information needed to leap over the empty space and commence volume traversal in the vicinity of meaningful data. The algorithm starts by projecting the volume into a *C*-buffer (Coordinate-buffer) which stores, at each pixel location, the object space coordinates of the first non-empty voxel visible from that pixel. For each change in the viewing parameters, the *C*-buffer is transformed accordingly. In the case of rotation the transformed *C*-buffer goes through a process of eliminating coordinates that may have become hidden [GR90]. The remaining values in the *C*-buffer serve as an estimate of the point where the new rays should start their volume traversal.

Space-leaping

The passage of a ray through the volume is two-phased. In the first phase the ray advances through the empty space searching for an object (see Figure 2.2a). In the second phase the ray integrates colors and opacities as it penetrates the object (in the case of multiple or concave objects these two phases can repeat). Commonly, the second phase involves one or a few steps, depending on the object's opacity. Since the passage of empty space does not contribute to the final image it is observed that skipping the empty space could provide significant speed up without affecting image quality. In some methods, space leaping is made possible by taking advantage of some coherency type described above.

So far we have seen methods that exploit some type of coherency to expedite volumetric ray casting. However, the most prolific and effective branch of volume rendering acceleration techniques involves the utilization of the fifth principle mentioned above: speeding up ray casting by providing efficient means to traverse the empty space.

The hierarchical representation (e.g., octree) decomposes the volume into uniform regions that can be represented by nodes in a hierarchical data structure [Sab88]. An adjusted ray traversal algorithm skips the (uniform) empty space by maneuvering through the hierarchical data structure [Lev90a]. It has also been observed that traversing the hierarchical data structure is inefficient compared to the traversal of regular grids. A combination of the advantages of both representations is the uniform buffer. The 'uniformity information' decoded by the octree can be stored in the empty space of a regular 3D raster. That is, voxels in the uniform buffer contain either a data value or information indicating to which size of empty octant they belong. Rays which are cast into the volume encounter either a data voxel, or a voxel containing

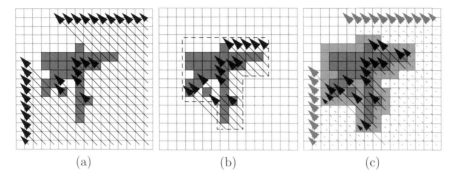

(a)   (b)   (c)

Figure 2.2   (a) The passage of rays through the volume where most of the time is spent on traversing empty space. (b) The data is surrounded by a bounding polyhedra and rays start tracing from its boundary. (c) Low-cost (e.g., integer) rays are traced in the empty space. They switch to high-cost rays when they encounter a voxel with its vicinity flag turned on.

"uniformity information" which instructs the ray to perform a leap forward that brings it to the first voxel beyond the uniform region [CS93]. This approach saves the need to perform a tree search for the appropriate neighbor – an operation that is the most time-consuming and the major disadvantage in the hierarchical data structure.

When a volume consists of one object surrounded by empty space, a common and simple method for skipping most of this empty space uses the well known technique of bounding-boxes. The object is surrounded by a tightly fit box (or other easy-to-intersect object such as sphere). Rays are intersected with the bounding object and start their actual volume traversal from this intersection point as opposed to starting from the volume boundary. The PARC (Polygon Assisted Ray Casting) approach [ASK92] strives to have a better fit by allowing a polyhedral envelope to be constructed around the object (see Figure 2.2b). PARC utilizes available graphics hardware to render the front faces of the envelope (to determine, for each pixel, the ray entry point) and the back faces (to determine the ray exit point). The ray is then traversed from entry to exit point. A ray that does not hit any object is not traversed at all.

It is obvious that the empty space does not have to be sampled – it has only to be crossed as fast as possible. Therefore, we have proposed [YCK92, Yag92] to utilize one fast and crude line algorithm in the empty space (e.g., a 3D integer-based 26-connected line algorithm) and another, slower but more accurate (e.g., a 6-connected integer or 3D DDA floating-point line algorithm), in the vicinity and interior of objects (see Figure 2.2c). The effectiveness of this approach depends on its ability to efficiently switch back and forth between the two line algorithms, and its ability to efficiently detect the proximity of occupied voxels. This is achieved by surrounding the occupied voxels by a one-voxel-deep 'cloud' of flag-voxels, that is, all empty voxels neighboring an occupied voxel are assigned, in a preprocessing stage, a special 'vicinity flag'. A crude ray algorithm is employed to rapidly traverse the empty space until it encounters a vicinity voxel. This flags the need to switch to a more accurate ray traversal algorithm. Encountering later an empty voxel (i.e., unoccupied and not carrying the vicinity flag) can signal a switch back to the rapid traversal of empty space.

The proximity-clouds method [CS93, ZKV92] is based on the extension of this idea even further. Instead of having a one-voxel-deep vicinity cloud this method computes, in a preprocessing stage, for each empty voxel, the distance to the closest occupied voxel. When a ray is sent into the volume it can either encounter an occupied voxel, to be handled as usual, or a 'proximity voxel' carrying the value n. This suggests that the ray can take a n-step leap forward, being assured that there is no object in the skipped span of voxels. The effectiveness of this algorithm is obviously dependent on the ability of the line traversal algorithm to efficiently jump an arbitrary number of steps [CS93].

2.3   PARALLEL AND DISTRIBUTED ARCHITECTURES

The viewing algorithms adopted for parallel implementations are many and varied. Both traditional direct volume rendering methods, namely feed-forward and backward-feed, and a hybrid approach were adapted for parallel processors. In the next three subsections we describe some of the existing parallel algorithms for volume rendering.

2.3.1   Parallel Forward Viewing Methods

Multiple-transformation methods and splatting have been commonly employed for parallel implementations. By converting the three-dimensional view matrix into a series of one-dimensional shears and scales along the orthogonal axis, both Schroeder and Salem [SS92] and Vezina, et al. [VFR92] implemented feed-forward rendering on SIMD processors. A one-dimensional shear leads to regular communication along the shear axis and hence the decomposition of the transformation into shears. In [VFR92] the implementation was conducted on a Maspar MP-1. Beams of voxels were provided to a toroidally connected processors. This implementation relies on the efficient interconnection network of the MP-1 for optimal communications performance. In the other implementation [SS91] no efforts were made to perform any explicit distribution or virtualization on the CM-2. Indirect addressing was employed and data exchange was avoided until the composition phase of the algorithm. This implementation however suffers from two disadvantages, namely, more one-dimensional resampling passes are required and perspective viewing is not handled.

Anupam, et al. [ABSS94] experimented with both image space and object space partitioning schemes for distributed volume rendering on a set of networked workstations. The images rendered by each workstation are composited to generate the final image.

Splatting is another reconstruction technique which has gained attention in the parallel volume rendering community. The earliest splatting implementation was conducted on a network of SUNs by Westover [Wes90]. Voxels are enumerated in a front-to-back or back-to-front order and a subset of these is sent to N^2 processes which are executed on a network of SUNs. These processes transform and splat the voxels onto image sheets which are then sent to N compositing processes.

Machiraju and Yagel implemented a similar splatting algorithm on a IBM Power Visualization System (PVS) [YM95]. In this method, shown in Figure 2.3, a computational scheme is utilized which allows very efficient transformations based on incremental vectorized computation. Also, the volume is statically divided into an ordered set of slabs (of slices). Each of the slices in a slab is independently transformed, shaded, splatted and composited with the existing local image. A tree-like algorithm is used to hierarchically combine all these local images to create the final image. Thus, inter-node communication is required only in this final stage. The amount of communication required is low and this implementation scales well with an increased number of processors.

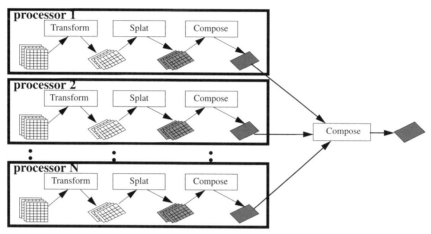

Figure 2.3 Parallel volume rendering by object space subdivision – each processor renders a sub-cube. The process is also pipelined and vectorized (in the transformation phase). The images resulting from each processor are composited to yield the final image.

In Neumann's implementation on the Pixel Planes 5 architecture [YNF+92] graphics processors transform and shade the voxels, while the rendering processors implement splatting and receive the requisite instruction stream from the graphics processors. Each rendering processor is assigned a subsection of the screen. Only voxels which map to that screen area are sent to this renderer. A sorting step is required for generating the splat instructions for appropriate renderers. A graphics processor waits for the a circulating token to reach it before it can send the next slice for rendering. While waiting, it transforms the next assigned slice. One disadvantage of this implementation is the sorting which is required for each of the slices.

The efficient shearing algorithm [LL94] was also parallelized, for a shared-memory architecture (Silicon Graphics Challenge) [Lac95] and on TMC CM-5 [AGS95]. In [Lac95], synchronization time is minimized by using dynamic load balancing and a task partition that minimizes synchronization events. The algorithm relies on hardware support for low-latency fine-grain communication and hardware caching to hide latency.

2.3.2   Parallel Backward Viewing Methods

Backward-feed or image space methods have received a lot of attention in the parallel volume rendering community. Neih and Levoy's [NL92] contribution lies in the development of a hybrid data distribution scheme. The screen is divided into several regions which are again subdivided into tiles. Each node of the DASH multicomputer is assigned a portion of the screen. If a node finishes ray-casting and finds another region undone, it grabs the next undone tile in a scanline order. To alleviate nonlocal access the volume is distributed in a round-robin fashion among the nodes. The efficient caching subsystem of the DASH multiprocessor is relied upon to fetch nonlocal data. In a similar approach, Anupam, et al. [ABSS94] distributed the volume rendering task among a set of networked workstations, acheiving high-performance computation in a low-cost environment.

Montani et al.'s implementation of a ray-tracer on the Intel iPSC/2 used a purely static data distribution scheme [MPS92]. The scanlines are divided among clusters of processors in an interleaved fashion. The entire volume data is replicated on all clusters with each node of the cluster getting a slab of slices. Rays are traced by each node with in its subvolume using a ray-dataflow approach, wherein a ray is split into several portions and each portion is traced individually. Later when each node is finished all these portions are combined to obtain the color. Such a scheme can lead to a load balanced and scalable implementation and the data distribution scheme maps well to the Hypercube interconnection network.

Fruhaff's implementation on a multiprocessor Silicon Graphics workstation [Fru92] is similar in spirit to Schroeder and Salem's implementation on CM-2. The volume is rotated along the viewing rays and then parallel rays are cast. A dynamic data distribution scheme is used to assign the slices to the various nodes. An efficient incremental transformation method is used for transforming each slice.

Corrie and Mackerras employed the Fujitsu AP1000 MIMD multiprocessor to implement a ray-caster [CM92a]. A master–slave paradigm was used to dynamically distribute square regions of pixels to slave cells. An adaptive distribution scheme is obtained by having the slave cells notify the master when they take more than their allocated time to render the assigned image. The master then subdivides the image region further and distributes the new sub-regions to idle cells. To support such a dynamic scheme the volume is replicated among clusters of neighboring cells.

The template-based viewing method [YK92] has been successfully implemented in [CU92] and [SS92] on SIMD machines. Both implementations are very similar. Parallel rays are traced in a lock step fashion by all nodes of the SIMD node. Each node is mapped to a voxel in both implementations. Shading, interpolation and compositing is done by each processor along the ray. After a set of rays have been completely traced, new rays are traced by conducting shifts along one axis.

We have designed and implemented three coherent algorithms on the Cray T3D [LY96a], which have proven to be extremely scalable, with scope for further improvement. These algorithms are primarily based on efficient utilization of local memory and attempt to hide the latency of locally unavailable objects. The irregularity and unpredictability of the problem at hand makes these features all the more difficult to achieve.

Recently, the CellFlow method [LYJ96, LY95], has been implemented on some distributed shared-memory architectures. It is based on exploiting coherency between frames in an animation sequence. Once the data is distributed among processors, it is observed that, if the animation is rather smooth, the amount of additional information needed for the next frame is small. We determined that instead of statically allocating parts of the volume to each processor, the local memory utilization could be optimized if only the required data were made locally available, that is, data which will be needed by a processor to generate its assigned portion of the screen. Depending on the local memory availability, this data allocation scheme can be extended to provide what is termed as frame-to-frame coherence, where data are allocated in such a way that a processor is self-sufficient in generating a number of slowly changing frames [LY96b] with no need for additional communication. If the animator happens to have the knowledge of subsequent screen positions, then the data needed for the next set of frames can similarly be fetched. This allows for effective overlapping of computation and communication (latency hiding) as well, because data required for the next set of frames may be fetched and be made available in local memory while the current set of frames is being generated.

2.3.3   Parallel Hybrid Methods

Hybrid methods have not drawn the same amount of attention as forward/backward feed methods. Only two reported implementations [YM95, WS93] and one recent work [LY96b] are known. Wittenbrink and Somani's [WS93] method is applicable to affine transformations. They decompose the transformation into a series of shears used to determine the address of a voxel in the transformed space. This address is used for interpolating in object space and obtaining the sample value. The advantage of this address computation scheme is that communication required for interpolation is nearest neighbor and regular. In the final stages another communication step is required for actually rearranging the transformed volume.

In [YM95], a hybrid method was implemented on the IBM Power Visualization System (PVS). The volume data is subdivided into sub-cubes and assigned to different processors. The transformed extents of these sub-cubes are determined in the image space. These image extents are then traversed in scanline order and interpolated in object space. An efficient inverse incremental transformation is employed to obtain points in object space.

Recently [LY96b], the Active Ray method, which exploits coherency in object space, was implemented. The data is divided into cells that are distributed randomly to processors. Rays are intersected with the cell boundaries and are placed in a queue associated with the cell they intersect first. These cells are brought into memory by demand in a front-to-back order. Rays queued at a cell that was brought into the processor's memory are advanced in the cell. They either stop due to opacity accumulation, or are queued at the cell they enter next. This hybrid method benefits from both the advantages of image order (e.g., early ray termination) and object order (e.g., regular space traversal) approaches.

The CellFlow method described above finds good application when subsequent screen positions are known a priori and works well for incremental rotations of the screen. We developed a method for exploiting frame-to-frame coherence in a more general way, i.e., for real-time animation where the screen positions are unpredictable. Several memory optimizations were made and a directory-based protocol was designed to optimize memory utilization further [LY96c]. It was seen that with sufficient local memory size to hold all the objects for a single frame, the data requirement for the next (close) frame was just 5% of the volume. No memory was assigned for static data allocation, objects migrated within the system, and the directory was used to trace an object's location. Latency hiding was achieved by stacking all the rays for which data needed to be fetched from other nodes (inactive rays), while rays for which all the required data were locally available (active rays) were traced to completion. Furthermore, our screen assignment scheme ensured that the nonavailable data at a node were always available from one of its neighboring nodes. We also devised a forwarding scheme which minimized network congestion, thus taking advantage of spatial coherency as well. The overall system provided enough generalization and independence from the underlying network. Considerable load balancing, sufficient latency hiding, network congestion control, and exploiting frame-to-frame coherency all combined to make this algorithm extremely scalable.

2.4 COMMERCIAL GRAPHICS HARDWARE

One of the most common resources for rendering is off-the-shelf graphics hardware. However, these polygon rendering engines seem inherently unsuitable to the task. Recently, some new methods have tapped into this rendering power either by utilizing texture mapping capabilities for rendering splats [Cra95, LH91], or by exploiting solid texturing capabilities to implement a slicing-based volume rendering [CCF94].

The *Volume Splatter* [YESK95] relies on the notion of a *fuzzy voxel* set which consists of a subset of the volume's voxels. For each voxel in the original volume, we evaluate a transfer function that maps the gradient and the density of the given voxel to an "importance" number. We include a voxel in the fuzzy set if it has a large enough "importance" value (above some user-defined threshold). Unlike previous methods, which choose the voxels for the set by segmentation methods, our approach chooses the voxels to be included by their contribution to the final image. This process, which effectively rejects all the voxels that contribute little or nothing to the final image, greatly reduces the burden placed on the rendering pipeline (see Figure 2.4b).

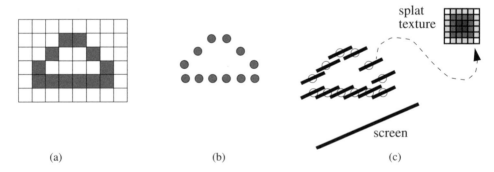

(a)   (b)   (c)

Figure 2.4 (a) The original data. (b) The set of extracted voxels. (c) Each voxel is associated a polygon that is texture-mapped with a splat texture. The polygons are always parallel to the screen plane.

The resulting subset of voxels, the fuzzy set, is ordered in the same fashion as the original volume: we hold slices of splats, where each slice contains rows of splats. The only difference is that the number of elements (splats) in each row may not be equal. Each row of splats is a sparse vector of original voxels; thus, for each splat in a row, we maintain its position in 3D space. In addition, we maintain the normal of each splat, which we calculate based on the information in all its 26 adjacent voxels.

The volume splatting algorithm takes as input a fuzzy set. It traverses the fuzzy set in a back-to-front order. For each member of the set, it renders a rectangle facing the viewer, textured with a splat texture. The splat texture contains an image of a fuzzy circle, with opaque center and transparent circumference (see Figure 2.4c). We also implemented a faster version of the rendering algorithm, in which, instead of rectangles, we render enlarged points on the screen. These points have constant opacity and therefore generate images with some visible artifacts; however, because points are very simple graphic primitives, this method supports higher rendering speeds.

We control the material properties of the splats; however, for reasons of speed, we vary only the opacity and diffuse reflection of the material for each splat. We define multiple light sources (infinite and local) and use the GL light routines to shade the splats. We exploit rendering hardware to provide real-time performance. Transforming the rectangles, scan-converting the textured rectangles, and compositing colors and opacities are performed by the graphics hardware.

The commercially available solid texturing hardware allows mapping of three-dimensional rasters (volumes) on polygons. These three-dimensional rasters (called 3D texture maps) are mapped onto polygons in 3D space using either zero-order or first-order interpolation. By rendering polygons slicing the volume and perpendicular to the view directions one generates a view of a rectangular volume dataset [CCF94]. Rendering these polygons from back to front and blending them into the frame buffer generates a correct image of the volume (see Figure 2.5).

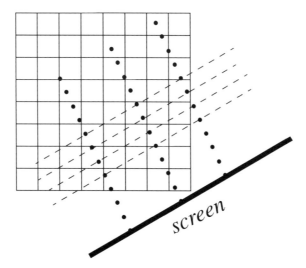

Figure 2.5 The equivalence of ray casting and slicing. The set composed of the ith sample along the rays form the ith slicing plane.

In order to use this hardware assisted volume rendering technique for volume deformation [KY95], we must compensate for the main difference between the two mapping techniques. In hardware assisted volume rendering we map a three-dimensional raster onto a polygon by interpolating the 3D raster coordinates of the polygon vertices. In other words, the mapping is linear across an entire polygon. In the ray deflection technique we do not perform any linear interpolations but map each point along a sight ray separately. We compensate for the linear interpolation by tessellating the polygons into smaller polygons. The tessellation limits the extent of the linear interpolation and provides better control of the deformation. This generates an obvious trade-off between the granularity of polygon tessellation and the visual quality of the resulting images. The finer the tessellation is, the more accurate our approximation of the deformation is, and the more computationally intensive the drawing process is.

2.5   FUTURE

The problem we are facing, of high-quality real-time rendering of high-resolution volumes has not been conquered as yet, nor does it seem to be heading towards a satisfactory solution in the near future. Nevertheless, the gap is narrowing and we seem to have gained some valuable lessons that will steer the field, in our opinion, in the following directions:

- The assembly and integration of existing methods into powerful algorithm that exploit various types of acceleration technique. One early example of this trend is the shear-warp algorithm that combines the work on shearing-based rendering [Han90], run-length encoding [RGC87], min-max pyramids [DH92], and multi-dimensional summed area tables.
- Parallel implementations on state-of-the-art distributed shared-memory machines, taking advantage of hardware caches and interleaved dedicated communication processors. Several examples of this trend are already available [LY95, LY96b, Ly96c].
- Migration of low-end volume rendering application into the PC domain, taking advantage of the recent giagantaic leap in graphics boards for PC.
- Increased utilization of existing general-purpose, affordable graphics engines with the final disappearance of special purpose volume engines. Some examples of this trend are in [CCF94], [Cra95], [LH91] and [YSW+96]. While the fastest known parallel implementations achieve close to real-time (10 frames per second) on expensive high-end parallel machines [Lac95], the same, or even slightly better performance is achieved on mid-range texture hardware [CCF94].

In addition to these we will see no doubt continued work in efficient storage schemes (e.g., directly rendered compressed data), exploitation of frame coherency, optimized illumination, rendering of colossal datasets, and various other unforeseen, and therefore so exciting, new ideas that promise to keep this field of exploration thriving with innovating activity in the future.

3

Accelerated Isocontouring of Scalar Fields

Chandrajit L. Bajaj and Valerio Pascucci
University of Texas, Austin

Daniel R. Schikore
Center for Applied Scientific Computing, LLNL

ABSTRACT

With the increasing size of typical 2D and 3D data, efficient computational methods are becoming increasingly crucial for achieving desired levels of interactivity. Computation of isocontours from scalar data is a particularly critical task for comprehensive visualization of volume data. In the case where the volume is discretized by a mesh of volumetric *cells*, the extraction of an isocontour consists of two primary phases: *triangulation* of a particular cell and the *search* for all intersected cells. In this chapter we will review and contrast the primary algorithmic approaches which have been suggested in the literature.

3.1 INTRODUCTION

Isocontouring is a widely used approach to the visualization of scalar data and an integral component of almost every visualization environment. Computation of isocontours has applications in visualization ranging from extraction of surfaces from medical volume data [Lor95] to computation of stream surfaces for flow visualization [van93]. Inherent in the selection of an isocontour, defined as $C(w) : \{\mathbf{x} | \mathcal{F}(\mathbf{x}) - w = 0\}$, is that only a selected subset of the data is represented in the result. In many applications, the ability to interactively modify the isovalue w while viewing the computed result is of great value in exploring the global scalar field structure. In fact, it has been observed in user studies that the majority of the time spent interacting with a visualization is in modifying the visualization parameters, *not* in changing the viewing

Data Visualization Techniques, Edited by C. Bajaj
© 1999 John Wiley & Sons Ltd

parameters [Hai91]. Hence there has been great interest in improving the computational efficiency of contouring algorithms.

We will focus on isocontouring of scalar fields which are defined over a piecewise cell decomposition rather than the more general case of implicit functions, although many issues cross over between the two input formats. In this situation, isocontouring algorithms can be characterized by three principal components:

- Cell Triangulation – Method of computation for determining the component of a contour which intersects a single cell.
- Cell Search – Method for finding all cells which contain components of the contour
- Cell Traversal – Order of cell visitation may be integrated with (or decided by) the cell search technique, however it affects the performance of the isocontour extraction algorithm

In the remainder of this chapter, we will discuss several isocontouring algorithms which address one or more of these components.

3.2   CELL TRIANGULATION

Cell triangulation concerns the approximation of the component of a contour which is interior to a given cell. Triangulation has two distinct components, *interpolation* to determine a set of points and normals, and *connectivity* to determine the local topology of the contour.

3.2.1   Interpolation

Cell-based contouring algorithms generally begin with a binary classification of each vertex of a given cell as *positive* (if greater than the isovalue) or *negative* (if less than or equal to the isovalue), which we will refer to as *black* and *white* vertices, respectively. For simplicity, most isocontouring algorithms adopt a simple interpolation approach along the edges of cells. Each edge which has one black vertex and one white vertex has exactly one intersection with the isocontour under the linear interpolation model, and this intersection point is easily computed as a linear combination of the endpoints of the edge. Any edge which has two vertices of the same color is appropriately disregarded, as the linear interpolation cannot intersect the isosurface if both endpoints are above or below the isovalue.

While linear interpolation along edges of cells is a widely used approach, interpolation is often the most computing-intensive portion of isocontour extraction. As data sizes increase and relative sizes of cells decrease, the effect of interpolating along cell edges is less noticeable. Other strategies have been developed to reduce this computational portion of isocontour approximation, such as selecting midpoints along intersected edges [MSS94]. Midpoint selection in grids of regular topology and uniform spacing has the added advantage that triangles extracted for the surface have relatively few facet orientations, resulting in large planar regions which are more easily coalesced to produce a simplified model of the isosurface for rapid rendering and compact representation.

A primary reason for applying linear interpolation in isocontouring is the fact that gradient information is often not present in the original data. If this is the case, gradient information may be estimated for the purpose of smooth surface shading by approximating gradients at the vertices and using linear interpolation of the gradient vector components within each cell. However, the ability of higher-degree interpolant and associated gradient estimators to accurately represent the underlying data is motivating work in this direction [MMMY96, BLM97].

3.2.2 Connectivity

The common approach of linear interpolation along cell edges is sufficient to obtain a sampling of points which lie on the surface, but the problem of connecting the points to form a surface still remains. A binary classification of the eight vertices of a regular cell leads to a total of $2^8 = 256$ possible configurations. Taking rotational symmetry into account, this can been reduced to 22 distinct cases [LVG80, Sri81]. Marching Cubes [LC87] further reduces the number of base cases by assigning complementary triangulation to complementary vertex configurations (*black* to *white*), resulting in 15 distinct colorings, for which connectivity information can be assigned, as shown in Figure 3.2. The full table of the 256 possible vertex configurations can easily be generated from this table of 15 cases.

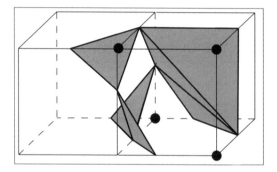

Figure 3.1 Topological inconsistency associated with the original marching cubes.

The use of complementary triangulations reduces the number of base cases, but also introduces a well known topological inconsistency on certain configurations of shared faces between cubes [Dur88], one case of which is illustrated in Figure 3.1. A number of techniques have been proposed which offer solutions to this inconsistency, which we group into two classes. The first class attempts only to provide *consistency* along cell faces, while the second class provides *correctness* with respect to a chosen model.

3.2.2.1 Consistent Connectivity

In cases in which the connectivity is not determined by the color of the vertices alone, continuous surfaces can be guaranteed by adopting a connectivity scheme which is consistent at a face shared by two adjacent cells.

Consistency may be achieved simply by subdividing each cell into tetrahedra and

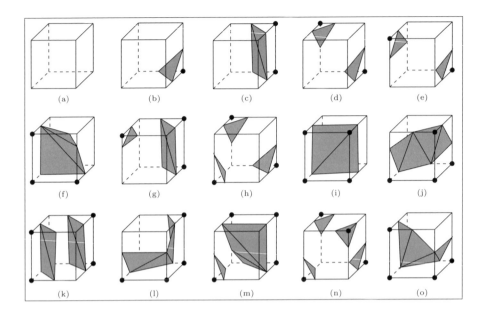

Figure 3.2 15 distinct vertex colorings.

using a linear interpolant within each tetrahedron [DK91]. An efficient approach to consistency is to adopt a consistent decision rule, such as sampling the function at the center of the ambiguous face to determine the local topology [WMW86].

3.2.2.2   Correct Connectivity

The core of the problem along shared cell faces lies in determining the topological connectivity of vertices which are colored the same but which lie diagonally across a face or body of a cell. A second class of connectivity solutions guarantees consistency on a shared face by ensuring correctness with respect to a particular data model.

Nielson and Hamann propose generating a consistent decision on connectivity by enforcing a topology which is correct with respect to the bilinear interpolant along the face [NH91]. Kenwright derives a similar condition for disambiguating the connectivity on the faces in terms of the gradient of the bilinear interpolant [Ken93]. Natarajan further enforces consistency with the trilinear interpolant for the case of ambiguities which are interior to a cell, which occur when diagonal vertices across the body of the cell are similarly colored but have no edge-connected path of vertices of the same color between them [Nat94]. Karron, et al. [KCM94] further discuss the proper treatment of criticalities in isocontouring, proposing a digital morse theory for describing the topological transitions of isocontours of scalar fields.

Zhou, et al. [ZCT95] make the point that a tetrahedral decomposition and linear approximation change the function and may still result in an incorrect, though consistent, topology. They propose that a tetrahedral decomposition may be used, provided that intersections along the introduced diagonals are computed for the cubic function which results from sampling the trilinear function across the diagonal of a cell, rather than applying linear interpolation along all edges.

Wilhelms and Van Gelder [WvG90, vGW94] provide a comprehensive review the topological considerations in extracting isosurfaces, and demonstrate that gradient heuristics applied at the vertices of a cell are necessary and sufficient to disambiguate the topology of functions which are quadratic.

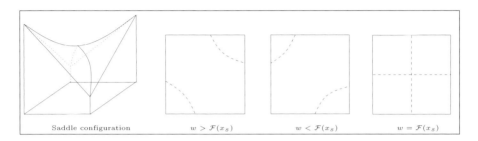

Figure 3.3   A two-dimensional bilinear saddle and its contour configurations.

The solution suggested by Natarajan [Nat94] is particularly attractive, due to its simplicity of implementation and design in enforcing consistency with the trilinear interpolant, a commonly used interpolant for 3D reconstruction and visualization. The situation on faces with colored vertices which are diagonally adjacent can be viewed in two dimensions as in Figure 3.3. The unique saddle point at coordinate $\mathbf{x_s}$ of the bilinear interpolant lies interior to the face, and the correct topology can be determined by evaluating the function at the saddle point and comparing it with the isovalue as shown. This topological consistency is carried out further by considering the unique saddle point of the full trilinear interpolant in addition to the six possible face saddles. A simple extension to a traditional case table requires sub-cases only for configurations which contain saddles. The sub-cases are indexed by the saddle point evaluations in order to determine a triangulation which is topologically consistent with the trilinear interpolant [Nat94].

Matveyev further simplifies the correctness in connectivity for the case of a regular cell by avoiding the explicit computation of the saddle points [Mat94]. With the observation that the asymptotes of a saddle in a regular cell are parallel to the coor-

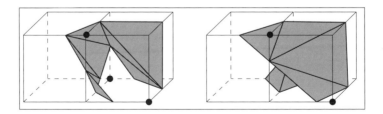

Figure 3.4   Two topologically consistent triangulations with respect to the shared face. Note that additional distinct configurations exist due to additional face saddles on the non-shared faces.

dinate axes, correct connectivity can be determined by sorting the intersections along an axial direction. The nature of the bilinear interpolant ensures that pairs in the sorting will be connected.

For the inconsistent case illustrated in Figure 3.1, several distinct topological triangulations are possible, two of which are illustrated in Figure 3.4.

3.3   CELL SEARCH

Because a contour only passes through a fraction of the cells of a mesh on average, algorithms which perform an exhaustive covering of cells are found to be inefficient, spending a large portion of time traversing cells which do not contribute to the contour. The straightforward approach of enumerating all cells to extract a contour leads to a high overhead cost when the surface being sought intersects only a small number of the cells.

Preprocessing of the scalar field permits the construction of search structures which accelerate the repeated action of isocontouring, allowing for increased interactivity during modification of the isovalue. Many preprocessing approaches and search structures have been presented, which are conveniently classified (similar to the classification presented in [LSJ96]) based on whether the search is in *domain* space or *range* space.

3.3.1   Domain Search

A straightforward search of the domain by enumerating all cells leads to an overhead cost of $O(n_c)$. In the case where few cells are intersected, this overhead cost is a dominant factor, leading to inefficient computation. A spatial hierarchy for accelerating the search process is a natural approach which has been explored by Wilhelms and Van Gelder [WvG92, WG90]. For space efficiency considerations, a partial octree decomposition was developed which groups all cells at the highest level and adaptively approximates the data through axis-aligned subdivisions which better approximate the data. At each level in the tree, *min* and *max* values for the cells contained in the subtree are stored, providing a means to efficiently discard large spatial regions in the search phase. An analysis presented in [LSJ96] suggests a worst-case computational complexity of $O(k + k \log \frac{n_c}{k})$, where k is the size of the output and n_c is the number of cells.

3.3.2   Range Search

A large number of search techniques in the recent literature perform the search for intersected cells in the *range* space of the function. As we are dealing only with scalar-valued functions, range space search techniques have the advantage of being independent of the dimension of the domain. In range space, each cell c is associated with the continuous set of values taken on by the function over the domain:

$$R(c) = [\min_{\mathbf{x} \in c} \mathcal{F}(\mathbf{x}), \max_{\mathbf{x} \in c} \mathcal{F}(\mathbf{x})]$$

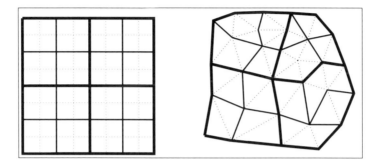

Figure 3.5 Spatial hierarchical cell decompositions for accelerating the search for isocontours.

There are two approaches for representing the range space, the 1D *value* space, in which each range $R(c)$ is considered as a segment, or interval, along the real line, and the 2D *span* space, in which each range $R(c)$ is considered as a point in 2D [LSJ96], as illustrated in Figure 3.6. While certain search structures are motivated by one geometric representation or another, others may be effectively visualized in either representation.

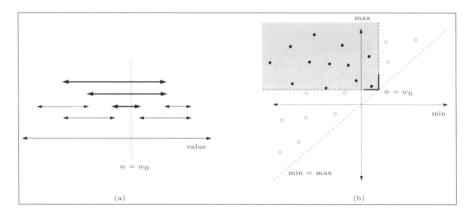

Figure 3.6 The (a) 1D value space and (b) 2D span space representations for range space searches.

Giles and Haimes introduce the use of lists of cells sorted by their minimum and maximum values to accelerate searching. In addition to forming two sorted lists of cells, the maximum cell range, Δw, is determined. Cells containing an isosurface of value w must have minimum value in the range $[w - \Delta w, w]$, which may be determined by binary search in the *min*-sorted array. This *active set* of cells is purged of cells whose range does not contain w. For small changes in w, the active list can be updated, rather than wholly recomputed, by adding and purging new candidate cells to/from the active list. In the worst case, the complexity remains $O(n_c)$.

Shen and Johnson [SJ95] describe the *Sweeping Simplices* algorithm, which builds on the *min-max* lists of Giles and Haimes and augments the approach with a hierarchical decomposition of the value space. The *min*-sorted list is augmented by pointers to the associated cell in the *max*-sorted list, and the *max*-sorted list is augmented by a "dirty bit." For a given isovalue, a binary search in the *min*-sorted list determines all cells with minimum value below the isovalue. Pointers from the minimum value list to the maximum value list are followed to set the corresponding dirty bit for each candidate cell. At the same time, the candidate cell with the largest maximum value which is less than the isovalue is determined. As a result, all marked (candidate) cells to the right of this cell in the maximum list must intersect the contour, as they have minimum value below the isovalue and maximum value above the isovalue. Optimizations may be performed when the isovalue is changed by a small delta. One *min-max* list is created for each level of a hierarchical decomposition of the *min-max* search space. The overall complexity remains $O(n_c)$ in the worst-case analysis.

Gallagher [Gal91] describes a span filtering algorithm, in which the entire range space of the scalar function is divided into a fixed number of *buckets*. Cells are grouped into buckets based on the minimum value taken on by the function over the cell. Within each bucket, cells are classified into one of several lists, based on the number of buckets which are *spanned* by the range of the cell. For an individual isovalue, cells which fall into a given bucket need only be examined if their span extends to the bucket which contains the isovalue. The worst case complexity remains $O(n_c)$.

Itoh and Koyamada [IK95] compute a graph of the extrema values in the scalar field. Every connected component of an isocontour is guaranteed to intersect at least one arc in the graph. Isocontours are generated by propagating contours from a seed point detected along these arcs. Noisy data with many extrema will reduce the performance of such a strategy. Livnat, et al. [LSJ96] note that in the worst case the number of arcs will be $O(n_c)$, and hence straightforward enumeration of the arcs is equivalent in complexity to enumeration of the cells.

Livnat, et al. describe a new approach which operates on the 2D *min-max span space* [LSJ96]. The span space representation of the cells is preprocessed using a *Kd-tree*, which allows $O(k + \sqrt{n_c})$ worst-case query time to determine the cells which intersect the contour, where k is the size of the output. It is reported that in the average case, k is the dominant factor, providing optimal average complexity.

The same authors, with Hansen [SHLJ96], have described a technique which demonstrates improved empirical results by using an $L \times L$ lattice decomposition of the span space, in addition to allowing for parallel implementation on a distributed memory architecture. With certain assumptions on the distributions of points in the span space, the worst-case query time improves to $O(k + \frac{n_c}{L} + \frac{\sqrt{n_c}}{L})$.

Several authors have recently demonstrated improved worst-case performance bounds with the use of the *interval tree* and *segment tree* data structures [BPS96, CMPS97, vK96]. Both structures provide a search complexity of $O(k + \log n_u)$, where n_u is the number of unique extreme values of the segments which define the tree and k is the number of reported segments intersected.

3.3.2.1   Range Queries

The fundamental isocontouring query concerns the enumeration of all cells c such that $w \in R(c)$ for the input isovalue w. In this section, four data structures supporting the range query are described in more detail, including discussion of storage complexity, time complexity for creation of the structure, and query complexity for reporting cells intersected given an isovalue.

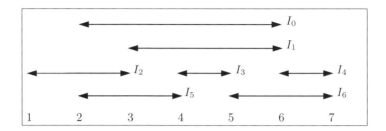

Figure 3.7   A set of segments representing cell ranges.

In the following sections we review the *interval tree, segment tree*, and *bucket* search structures as applied to the contour query problem described. Example search structures are illustrated for the input set of intervals shown in Figure 3.7. For each search structure, the complexity measures are based on the insertion of n_s cells (value space intervals) into the search structure. In the case where interval endpoints are taken from a small set of values (such as a limited set of the integers), the number of unique interval values is called n_u.

3.3.2.2   Interval Tree

An *interval tree* is made up of a binary tree over the set of interval *min/max* values [McC85]. Each internal node holds a *split value s*, with which intervals are compared during insertion into the tree. If the interval is entirely *less than* the split value it is recursively inserted into the left subtree, while intervals *greater than* the split value are recursively inserted into the right subtree.

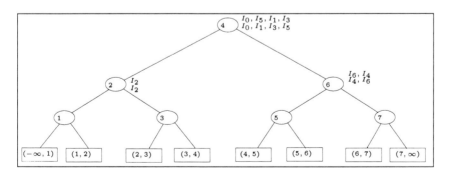

Figure 3.8   Interval tree for the intervals given in Figure 3.7.

In the case where the interval spans the split value ($min < s < max$), the recursion terminates and the given interval is stored at the current node. Each node maintains two lists of spanning cells. The first list is stored in increasing order by the *min* value, the second in decreasing order by the *max* value. Because the intervals are not split in the recursive insertion, each interval is stored only twice, and the storage complexity is $O(n_s)$.

3.3.2.3 Segment Tree

A segment tree also consists of a binary search tree over the set of *min* and *max* values of all the seed cells [Meh84, Mul94]. The primary difference from the interval tree is the manner in which the segments are stored. Nodes in a segment tree form a multi-resolution hierarchy of intervals, with the root representing the infinite line, and with each node dividing the parent interval at a split value (see Figure 3.9). When a segment is inserted into the tree, it is recursively split and propagated downward in the tree, to be inserted into the group of nodes whose intervals collectively sum to the entire range of the segment. Each segment identifier will be stored at most $O(\log n_u)$ times, where $\log n_u$ is the height of the tree, resulting in a worst-case storage complexity of $O(n_s \log n_u)$ in the improbable case that all *min-max* values are distinct, and all intervals filter all the way down to the leaves. The query complexity for reporting the k intersected cells for a given isovalue w is $O(k + \log n_u)$.

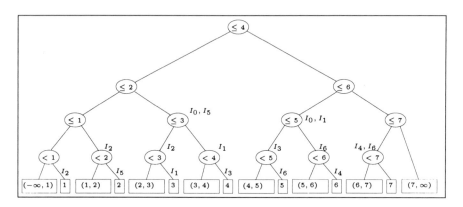

Figure 3.9 Segment tree for the segments given in Figure 3.7.

3.3.2.4 Bucket Search

Much of the scientific data that we are concerned with comes in the form of integer values in a small range. For example, Computed Tomography (CT) data generally have a 12-bit integer range of values. This regular subdivision allows a simple bucket search strategy with $n_u - 1$ buckets each representing a unit interval $(h, h + 1)$. For each cell, an identifier is stored in each bucket which is spanned by the cell. Clearly, the worst-case storage complexity of this strategy is $O(n_s n_u)$, which may be infeasible in the case in which all cells are stored. Given the approach of forming a small set of seed cells, such a technique may prove feasible, with the added benefit of allowing intersected cells to be reported in $O(k)$ time, linear in the number of reported cells.

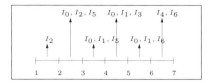

Figure 3.10   Bucket search structure for the intervals given in Figure 3.7.

3.3.2.5   Search Structure Discussion

In this section we discuss the storage cost of each of the three presented search structures. Table 3.1 summarizes the theoretical space and query complexities.

Search Structure	Storage Complexity	Query Complexity
Interval Tree	$O(n_s)$	$O(k + \log n_u)$
Segment Tree	$O(n_s \log n_u)$	$O(k + \log n_u)$
Bucket	$O(n_s n_u)$	$O(k)$

Table 3.1   Comparison of the theoretical complexities of the three search structures for performing an interval query.

3.4   CELL TRAVERSAL

The order in which cells are visited can impact the efficiency of contouring algorithms in several ways. Coherent traversal algorithms, such as a regular traversal scheme or contour propagation (breadth first traversal of a connected component), can potentially be implemented more efficiently than a random cell visitation order. One issue is the efficiency of avoiding recomputation (recomputing intersection along shared edges of cells). Through regular traversal and contour propagation, information can be saved more efficiently than in a random order visitation which is required by some cell search techniques.

3.4.1   Contour Propagation

Contour propagation [AFH80, HB94, IK95, BPS96] is a surface tracking method which is based on continuity of the scalar field, and hence of the isocontours derived from the field. Given a single *seed cell* on a connected component of a contour, the entire component is traced by breadth-first traversal through the face-adjacencies. The traversal is terminated when a cell which has already been processed is met again, which is usually determined by a set of *mark* bits, which indicate for each cell whether processing has taken place. The procedure is illustrated in Figure 3.11. In a contour propagation framework, as in a marching order traversal, optimization can be performed based on the fact that with each step, information from adjacent cells is available which can be used to avoid recomputation. In addition, the extracted contours are more easily transformed into representations such as triangle strips for efficient storage and rendering.

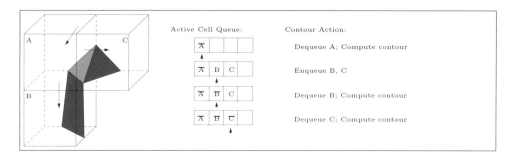

Figure 3.11 Illustration of contour propagation. The active surface is traced through adjacent cells.

Cignoni et al. [CDM+94] introduce a limited propagation scheme for regular grids based on a "checkerboard" seed set, as illustrated in Figure 3.12. By selecting a regular pattern of cells, it is guaranteed that all contours will intersect a black or grey cell. Modified contour propagation rules are applied to reach white cells from the selected black or grey cells. Determining the seed set requires very little computation, thus preprocessing is essentially limited to building the range search structure, in this case an interval tree.

Figure 3.12 Illustration of the "checkerboard" approach to sufficient seed sampling. Black cells are on the checkerboard, while a number of grey cells are also required in the seed set.

3.4.2 Seed Set Construction

Several of the cell search techniques presented above depend upon a subsequent cell traversal algorithm such as contour propagation. The use of a subsequent cell traversal algorithm allows a reduction in the size of the search structure, because a cell which will be processed by *traversal* need not be entered into the primary search structure. The traversal stage can thus be considered a secondary search phase.

Propagation from seed cells requires a sufficient subset of cells which guarantee that every connected component for any arbitrary isovalue intersects at least one cell in the subset, called a *seed set*. A general definition of seed sets and a framework for the construction of seed sets is presented in [BPS96].

3.4.2.1   Optimal Seed Sets

In [vvB$^+$97], the theory of optimal seed sets is discussed, which suggests that optimal (minimal) seed sets can be constructed in time which is polynomial in the number of cells, though the cost for minimal seed sets remains prohibitive for most cases.

The cost of implementation and computation for optimal seed sets is generally restrictive for all but the smallest of input meshes. Therefore, considerable work has been devoted to approximation algorithms. Algorithms for computing "good" seed sets are free to balance the desire for small (close to optimal) seed sets with the competing desire for low space/time complexity. As a result, seed set approaches can be tailored to suit a wide variety of settings and applications, depending on the available resources that can be dedicated to the computation. We shall review a selected subset of seed set construction algorithms.

3.4.2.2   Extrema Graphs

Itoh and Koyamada [IK95] introduce the use of *extrema graphs* for accelerating the search for isocontours. They observe that any closed contour must enclose an extremum of the scalar field, or be constant (or empty) within. By combining a search along a graph of the extreme points with a search of the boundary cells of the mesh, it is assured that at least one cell for each connected component of an isocontour is found. Cells extracted in this search are used as seed cells for an isocontour tracking algorithm, similar to the slicing algorithm described by Speray and Kennon [SK90].

3.4.2.3   Volume Thinning

Extending the extrema graph approach, Itoh, et al. [IYK96] have applied image thinning techniques to progressively remove from a volume mesh cells which are not necessary in the "skeleton" of the function. Cells which are on the current boundary are iteratively visited, and may be removed subject to conditions on the connectivity of the neighboring cells that remain in the mesh. They report that the cells extracted by volume thinning are significantly fewer than those extracted using extrema graphs, partially due to the fact that boundaries are no longer considered as a special case. Furthermore, the computational complexity of volume thinning is virtually independent of the number of extrema, and thus the thinning approach results in faster preprocessing in many cases.

3.4.2.4   Greedy Climbing

For computation of a nearly optimal seed sets Bajaj, et al. [BPS97b] develop a greedy technique which progressively covers the domain with seed cells by explicitly computing the coverage of each seed cell introduced. This *climbing* algorithm can be applied to both regular and unstructured grids of any cell type provided that the appropriate function R is given which computes the range of a cell or face.

The algorithm begins by considering the universal seed set S consisting of all cells c. Processing continues by iteratively selecting a cell in the seed set and tracing the set of all contours from the selected cell, effectively performing contour propagation for an interval of values. During the interval propagation, cells which are found to be unnecessary can be removed from the seed set. Figure 3.13 (Plate 12) illustrates the selection and removal process.

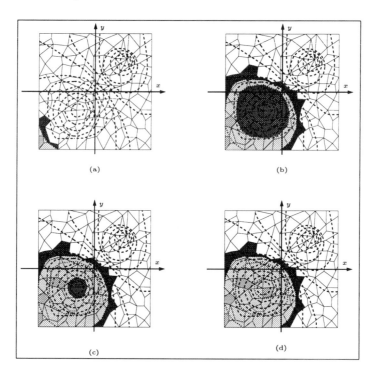

Figure 3.13   Greedy climbing approach to seed cell selection. Grey cells represent the selected seed cells. Yellow cells have been processed and removed from consideration, while red cells represent the current *front* of cells from which the next seed cell will be chosen. (See also color Plate 12)

3.4.2.5   Sweep Filtering

Bajaj, et al. [BPS97b] present a seed selection algorithm with simple selection criteria, motivated by practical considerations when dealing with extremely large data. The seed selection is conceptually easiest to understand as a sweep of the cells in a particular direction. The algorithm has the property that selected seeds fall on the extrema of the contours in the given sweep direction. Detection of contour extrema is based on a simple comparison of the gradient within each cell and its immediate neighbors. With such a seed set, contouring may be performed coherently and efficiently by executing a contouring sweep, with only a slice of data required to be resident in memory at any given time, resulting in efficient computation for visualization of large out-of-core datasets.

The seed selection stage is illustrated as a left-to-right sweep in Figure 3.14. Conceptually, the sweep line l is moved from left to right to determine the order in which cells are processed. Note that this ordering is not required by the selection algorithm, and so cells which are stored in main memory can be processed in any order, or even in parallel. When a cell c is met which contains a local maximum of an isocontour along the sweep direction $\vec{l}_\perp$, the cell c is added to the seed set.

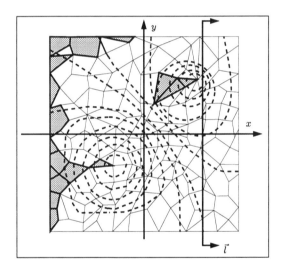

Figure 3.14   One-pass seed selection by forward sweep.

Sweep filtering requires $O(n_c)$ time for considering each cell, and no additional storage beyond that of the extracted seed set (and the portion of the mesh kept in memory). In addition to facilitating out-of-core computation, the sweep filtering approach provides an extremely efficient method for computing a small seed set. Moreover, due to the local criteria for seed selection, cells may be considered in any order, allowing for parallel implementation with little or no communication overhead during the preprocessing.

3.4.2.6   Responsibility Propagation

In earlier work, Bajaj, et al. [BPS96] described a plane sweep approach to seed set computation for regular grids. Results from the *responsibility propagation* algorithm fall between the general sweep filtering and the contour climbing. Processing of cells

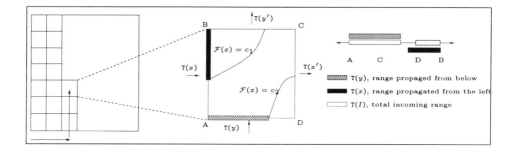

Figure 3.15 Illustration of responsibility propagation. Each cell processes input responsibilities and produces output responsibilities.

is performed in a regular traversal order, with ranges of responsibility propagated along the directions of the traversal. Illustrated in Figure 3.15, the traversal order is left-to-right and bottom-to-top. *Incoming* responsibility ranges are denoted $T(x)$ and $T(y)$, and computed propagated responsibilities are $T(x')$ and $T(y')$. Propagated responsibilities are computed using set arithmetic on the incoming responsibilities.

The *range propagation* method for selecting seed cells requires $O(n^{(d-1)/d})$ storage to maintain the propagated ranges for a sweep line or plane, where d is the dimension of the regular grid.

3.5 HIERARCHICAL AND OUT-OF-CORE PROCESSING

Extremely large data often require special care and processing. Two approaches in particular have been explored with respect to contouring of extremely large scalar fields.

Zhou, et al. [ZCK97] describe a hierarchical tetrahedral representation for volume data and discuss an approach to adaptive isocontouring from the multi-resolution volume representation. The hierarchy is constructed by recursive application of a set of three tetrahedron "splitting" rules. Isosurfaces can be extracted from this at a user-defined level of detail.

Chiang and Silva [CS97] use an I/O-optimal interval tree to perform efficient contouring of data which cannot be stored in primary memory. Results have indicated that isocontouring can be performed on data residing in secondary storage, so that the I/O operations required are not the limiting factor of the computation. The only primary memory required includes a small constant amount to store a portion of the mesh and storage for the isosurface being constructed.

3.6 SUMMARY

A key to efficient computation is in exploiting coherence. The isocontouring approaches described above can be loosely classified and analyzed based on the coherence which is exploited.

Spatial Coherence – We assume a minimum of C^0 continuity in our scalar field. Continuity along shared cell faces is exploited by many contouring approaches described above. The octree decomposition exploits spatial coherence in a hierarchical manner. As should be expected, the analysis in [LSJ96] reveals that the complexity gain breaks down when the spatial frequency is high, forcing large portions of the octree to be traversed.

Range Space Coherence – Searches in range space have demonstrated improved worst-case query complexity with performance which is independent of spatial frequency. Such advances, however, come at the cost of decreased ability to exploit spatial coherence. Assuming a continuous scalar field over a cell representation, cells which are spatially adjacent also overlap in the value space for the range of the shared face. However, the construction of value space search structures such as the interval tree and segment tree is completely independent of assumptions such as scalar field continuity. While this may be an advantage in the case where discontinuous fields or disjoint groups of cells are considered, for most purposes it means that spatial coherence is underutilized.

In general, domain-space and range-space searches exploit coherence in one sense by sacrificing coherence in another. The seed set approaches are best understood as a hybrid of spatial and value-space approaches, with the goal and result of exploiting both range-space and domain-space coherence.

The approach is based on a fragmentation of the search for intersected cells into *range-space* and *domain-space* phases, taking advantage of coherence in both. Range-space searches exhibit improved worst-case complexity bounds due to their independence from the spatial frequencies of the input data. By adopting *contour propagation* to compute each connected component, full advantage of spatial coherence during cell traversal is realized. Contour propagation also has the advantage of requiring only one *seed cell* for each connected component from which to begin tracing the contour, allowing for a much smaller search structure compared to algorithms which must search over the entire set of cells.

3.7 FUTURE DIRECTIONS

The use of interval tree and segment tree data structures has reduced the cost of searching for intersected cells to the point that contouring cost is highly dominated by the triangulation phase, and principally by the interpolation along mesh edges. Future avenues for interactive isocontouring will include improved approximate and hierarchical contouring algorithms. Hierarchical algorithms which are progressive will be developed, allowing computation to proceed at a specified rate for effective interactive use in real-time environments.

Another promising direction in making isocontouring more useful is through automated isovalue selection processes. Quantitative user interfaces such as the Contour Spectrum [BPS97a] both aid the user in selecting relevant isovalues and provide a framework within which the relevance of isovalues can be directly computed, removing from the user much of the need for blindly exploring the space of isosurfaces.

4

Surface Interrogation: Visualization Techniques for Surface Analysis

Stefanie Hahmann

Laboratoire de Modélisation et Calcul
Université de Grenoble, France

ABSTRACT

Surface interrogation is of central importance for CAD and Computer Graphics applications. Wherever free form surfaces are used, they often need to be analyzed with respect to different aspects like, for example, visual pleasantness, technical smoothness, geometric constraints or surface intrinsic properties. The various methods, which are presented in this paper, can be used to detect surface imperfections, to analyze shapes or to visualize different forms.

4.1 INTRODUCTION

The geometric modeling of free form curves and surfaces is of central importance for sophisticated CAD/CAM systems, for many computer graphics applications, and in the field of numerical simulations based on finite element techniques. Surface interrogation methods find their origin in the CAD/CAM technologies which require high-quality surfaces. A wide variety of surface formulations have been developed to satisfy these requirements (see, for example, [BFK84], [Far88] and [HL92] for an overview).

Surfaces in automobile design need to be smooth and need to have good reflection characteristics. Ship hull design necessitates minimal energy surfaces. NC processing has special requirements for surfaces. Milling machines limit the amount of curvature radii of the surface. The flow behavior of surfaces in aerodynamic studies (turbine blade, air plane wings,...) depends on the continuity and smoothness of the underlying surface. A lot of other examples can be found in order to underline that surface interrogation is a key issue in the geometric design process.

4.1.1   Purposes of Surface Interrogation

Surface interrogation methods provide important tools in analyzing the intrinsic shape and curvature properties of parametric surfaces. They frequently reveal anomalous behavior which is not immediately apparent in simple isoparametric curve digitizations or in high-resolution shaded images.

While defining parametric surfaces interpolatory or boundary constraints need to be satisfied (for example, fitting surfaces to arrays of discrete points, generation of blend surfaces). But they often introduce undesired surface behaviors due to the poor control over their many degrees of freedom. Analysis tools are needed for detecting such surface imperfections.

Most applications in industrial design require

- smoothness
- shape fidelity

The need for fair or smooth surface shapes can be motivated by different considerations. In automobile design aesthetic aspects are dominating, while in aircraft and ship design aerodynamics and hydrodynamic constraints must be satisfied.

The smoothness is therefore related to a lot of different surface features, like

- continuity between adjacent patches in tangents and curvature
- curvature distribution
- flat points
- convexity

which are driven directly from the surface differential geometry. Aesthetically smooth surfaces must not have

- bumps, dents (surface irregularities)

which can be described mathematically as small curvature variations. Smooth surfaces also need to have

- good light reflection behavior.

More technical considerations in surface design are NC milling verification, robot collision detection, and so on. The recognition of surface imperfections, like

- exceed of curvature bounds
- high variation of curvature

can prevent failure of tool-path generation algorithms for example.

The detection of surface imperfections like those mentioned above is one task of surface interrogation methods. Some of them are surveyed in Hagen, et al. [HHS+92]. Another application, not necessarily disjoint from the first one, is the visualization of differential geometry surface features like

- curvature behavior (principal curvature, Gaussian curvature)
- parabolic lines
- isolines
- lines of curvature
- umbilics
- geodesic lines

They provide tools for a detailed analysis of the intrinsic geometry of the surface with various applications and they facilitate the design of surfaces (see, for example, Beck, et al. [BFH86]).

4.1.2 Overview

The main purpose of this chapter is to give an overview of surface interrogation methods. Owing to the large number of different applications of surface interrogation one feels tempted to divide these techniques into two main subgroups: techniques for *visualizing surface features* and techniques for *detecting and remedying unexpected surface characteristics*. But there are some methods, like isoline extraction, which thwart this plan because they belong to both groups. On one hand they are used to visualize surface features, to increase the 3D-understanding, and to analyze the intrinsic geometry of the surface, and on the other hand they interrogate the smoothness/fairness of surfaces and their technical suitability for NC processing. Various visualization techniques identify unwanted surface features, but no method is optimal for all applications.

In order to keep readers free in their choice of the appropriate surface interrogation method for a specific application, the chapter will be structured as follows. Before we turn to a detailed presentation of surface analysis techniques, we will briefly give a review of differential geometry in Section 4.2. In Section 4.3 the presentation of each surface interrogation method is accompanied by examples of applications.

4.2 REVIEW OF DIFFERENTIAL GEOMETRY

The differential geometry of surfaces is fundamental for the following sections. There is much literature on this subject ([dC76, Eis76, Kre59, Boe93]), so we only summarize the relevant definitions here.

Let us consider a surface in real euclidean 3-space $\mathbb{R}^3$, given in parametric representation

$$X = X(u, w) = \begin{bmatrix} x(u, w) \\ y(u, w) \\ z(u, w) \end{bmatrix}, \quad (u, w) \in G \subset \mathbb{R}^2 \tag{4.1}$$

where $X \in C^r(G)$. To avoid undefined normal vectors, we assume a regular parameterization, i.e., the partial derivative vectors $X_1 := \frac{\partial X}{\partial u}$, $X_2 := \frac{\partial X}{\partial w}$ are linear independent in G. The unit normal vector of $X(u, w)$ can then be defined as

$$N(u, w) := \frac{X_1 \times X_2}{\|X_1 \times X_2\|} \tag{4.2}$$

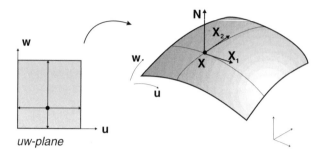

Figure 4.1   Parametric surface.

where $\times$ denotes the cross product. There are two important geometric structures defined by the surface which completely characterize the shape of the surface: the first and second fundamental forms.

The two fundamental forms: The *first fundamental form I* is also called the metric form, because it allows us to make measurements on the surface, such as lengths, areas and angles between two curves on the surface. A regular curve $[u(t), w(t)]^T$ in the uw-plane defines a regular curve $X(u(t), w(t))$ on the surface. The (squared) arc element of this curve is then given by

$$ds^2 = dX \cdot dX = g_{11}du^2 + 2g_{12}dudw + g_{22}dw^2 \tag{4.3}$$

where $g_{ij} = X_i \cdot X_j$, $(i, j = 1, 2)$, and is called *first fundamental form* $I := ds^2$. The subscripts denote partial derivatives. The arc element ds is a geometric invariant, i.e., it does not depend on the particular parameterization chosen for the representation (4.1) of the surface.

While the first fundamental form I is defined as the dot product of the infinitesimal displacement of any curve on the surface dX by itself, the *second fundamental form II* is defined as the dot product of dX of any surface curve and infinitesimal variation dN of the surface unit normal N along such a curve:

$$II = -dX \cdot dN = h_{11}du^2 + 2h_{12}dudw + h_{22}dw^2 \tag{4.4}$$

with $h_{ij} = -X_i \cdot N_j = X_{ij} \cdot N$, $i, j = 1, 2$. The second fundamental form II together with the first fundamental form I allows us to compute the surface curvatures.

Surface curvatures: The family of planes containing the surface normal N at a given point P cuts the surface in a family of *normal section curves C* for that point.

Let t be the tangent vector of the normal section curve C at P. The *normal curvature* κ of the surface is defined as the curvature of the normal section curve and can be calculated by utilizing differentiation of equation $N \cdot t = 0$ along C with respect to arc length:

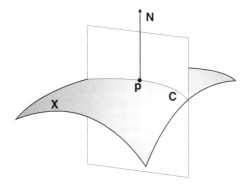

Figure 4.2 Normal section curves.

$$\kappa = \kappa(\lambda) = -\frac{dt}{ds} \cdot N = t \cdot \frac{dN}{ds} = \frac{dX}{ds} \cdot \frac{dN}{ds} = -\frac{II}{I} = -\frac{h_{11} + 2h_{12}\lambda + h_{22}\lambda^2}{g_{11} + 2g_{12}\lambda + g_{22}\lambda^2} \quad (4.5)$$

where $\lambda = dw/du$ specifies the direction of the curve, see Figure 4.2. The negative sign in equation (4.5) gives positive curvature if the center of curvature lies opposite to the direction of the surface normal (convex). In the special case where $g_{11} : g_{12} : g_{22} = h_{11} : h_{12} : h_{22}$, the normal curvature κ is independent of λ. Points with that property are called *umbilical points*.

In general, at each point κ varies with each direction $\lambda = dw/du$. The extreme values κ_1 and κ_2 of $\kappa(\lambda)$ occur at the roots λ_1 and λ_2 of

$$\det \begin{vmatrix} \lambda^2 & -\lambda & 1 \\ g_{11} & g_{12} & g_{22} \\ h_{11} & h_{12} & h_{22} \end{vmatrix} = 0. \quad (4.6)$$

The extreme values κ_1 and κ_2 satisfy the two simultaneous equations

$$\begin{aligned} (h_{11} + \kappa g_{11})du + h_{12} + \kappa g_{12})dw &= 0 \\ (h_{12} + \kappa g_{12})du + h_{22} + \kappa g_{22})dw &= 0 \end{aligned} \quad (4.7)$$

and are therefore the roots of

$$\det \begin{vmatrix} \kappa g_{11} + h_{11} & \kappa g_{12} + h_{12} \\ \kappa g_{12} + h_{12} & \kappa g_{22} + h_{22} \end{vmatrix} = 0. \quad (4.8)$$

κ_1 and κ_2 are called *principal curvatures* ($\kappa_1 = \kappa_{\max}$, $\kappa_2 = \kappa_{\min}$). The corresponding directions λ_1, λ_2 define directions in the uw-plane and the corresponding directions in the tangent plane are called *principal curvature directions*. They are always orthogonal except at umbilical points ($\kappa_1 = \kappa_2$) where the principal directions are undefined. A special umbilical point is a *flat point* ($\kappa_1 = \kappa_2 = 0$) where the surface becomes locally flat. Umbilical points are also called spherical points, since the surface locally approximates a sphere at those points.

The net of lines that have the principal directions at all their points is called net of *lines of curvature*. It can be calculated by integrating equations (4.7).

Gaussian and mean curvature: The two principal curvatures κ_1 and κ_2 are given by

$$
\begin{aligned}
\kappa_1 &= H + \sqrt{H^2 - K} \\
\kappa_2 &= H - \sqrt{H^2 - K}
\end{aligned}
\tag{4.9}
$$

where K is the *Gaussian curvature* and H is the *mean curvature*. They are defined by

$$
\begin{aligned}
K &= \frac{h_{11}h_{22} - h_{12}^2}{g_{11}g_{22} - g_{12}^2} \\[2mm]
H &= -\frac{2g_{12}h_{12} - g_{11}h_{22} - g_{22}h_{11}}{2(g_{11}g_{22} - g_{12}^2)}
\end{aligned}
\tag{4.10}
$$

$$
\begin{aligned}
K &= \kappa_1\kappa_2 \\[1mm]
H &= \frac{\kappa_1 + \kappa_2}{2}
\end{aligned}
\tag{4.11}
$$

If κ_1 and κ_2 are of the same sign, i.e., if $K > 0$, the point under consideration is called *elliptic* (for example: ellipsoid). If κ_1 and κ_2 have different signs, i.e., if $K < 0$, the surface point is called *hyperbolic*. If either κ_1 or κ_2 is zero, the Gaussian curvature is zero and the surface point is called *parabolic*.

4.3   SURFACE INTERROGATION METHODS

4.3.1   Isolines

Isolines are an interrogation tool with a wide variety of applications. They provide powerful intuition in understanding curved surfaces. They help in analyzing surface characteristics and they are used to visualize the distribution of scalar quantities over the surface. Isolines are lines of a constant characteristic value on the surface. The visualization of a certain number of isolines, with respect to an even distribution of the characteristic values, allows us to study the behavior of these values.

4.3.1.1   Contour Lines

Contour lines are planar lines on the surface which are all parallel to a fixed reference plane. Closed contour lines indicate maxima and minima of the surface with respect to the direction given by the plane's normal vector (see [HN82], or [BFH86]. Saddle points appear as "passes". The contour lines only cross in the exceptional case of a contour at the precise level of a saddle point. Nackman [Nac84] describes systematically the distribution of other critical points on a surface. A disadvantage of contour lines is the fact that they are costly to compute. Several surface contouring methods exist, which are sometimes dependent of the specific surface formulation (see [Pet84], [SR85] and [LF84]). Hartwig and Nowacki [HN82] propose subdividing the surface into sufficient small pieces which are then approximated by bilinear surfaces. Then the contour lines can easily be computed.

4.3.1.2 Parabolic Lines

Parabolic lines are mentioned here as an example for isolines of a constant function value over the surface. Parabolic lines are lines of zero Gaussian curvature on the surface. They divide the surface into elliptic and hyperbolic regions and they reflect therefore the local curvature behavior of a surface. Parabolic lines are special Gaussian curvature lines.

Figure 4.3 Parabolic lines, left; Gaussian curvature isolines, right.

The idea of plotting parabolic lines is not new. As reported by Hilbert and Cohen-Vossen [HCV52], Felix Klein[1] speculated that the artistic beauty of the statue Apollo Belvedere "... was based on certain mathematical relations...". But he couldn't discover any general law confirming his thesis. Nevertheless Gaussian isolines plotted on an engineering surface give the designer insight into shape and can detect unwanted curvature behavior, such as changes in the sign of the Gaussian curvature.

4.3.2 Light Reflection Methods

The light reflection methods all simulate the special reflection behavior of light sources or light lines on the surface. Owing to the intuitive understanding that everybody has when they observe light reflections, these methods are very effective in detecting surface irregularities. They are therefore very well suited to testing the fairness of surfaces. Because the surface normals are involved in the computation of these lines, they also can be used to visualize first-order discontinuities, such as tangent discontinuities.

---

[1] Felix Klein, German mathematician (1849–1925)

4.3.2.1   Reflection Lines

The reflection line method determines unwanted dents by emphasizing irregularities
in the reflection line pattern of parallel light lines.

Let $X(u, w)$ be a representation of the surface to investigate, and let $N(u, w)$ be
the unit normal vector of the surface. Furthermore a *light line* L is given in parameter
form:

$$L(t) = L_0 + t \cdot \vec{s}$$

where $t \in \mathbb{R}$, and point A is a fixed eye point.

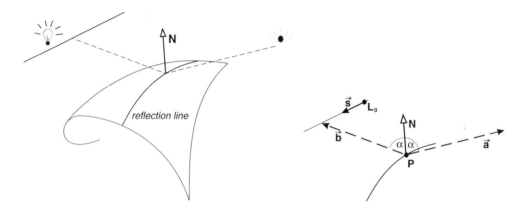

Figure 4.4   Reflection line method.

The reflection line is the projection of the line L on the surface X, which can be seen
from the eye point A, if the light line L is reflected on the surface, see Figure 4.4.
From geometric dependencies the following reflection condition is easily seen:

$$\frac{\vec{a}}{\|\vec{a}\|} + \frac{\vec{b}}{\|\vec{b}\|} = 2 \left(N(u, w) \cdot \frac{\vec{b}}{\|\vec{b}\|} \right) N(u, w)$$

$$= 2 \left(N(u, w) \cdot \frac{\vec{a}}{\|\vec{a}\|} \right) N(u, w)$$

where $\vec{a} = P - A$, $\vec{b} = L - P$. To evaluate the surface we use a set of reflection lines
with direction $\vec{s}$ and step along each curve of the set. For a fixed eye point A, the
following nonlinear system of equations for the unknown parameters u and w of the
reflection point P has to be determined:

$$\vec{b} + \lambda \vec{a} = 2 \left(N(u, w) \cdot \vec{b} \right) N(u, w) \quad \text{with} \quad \lambda := \frac{\|\vec{b}\|}{\|\vec{a}\|} \tag{4.12}$$

These three nonlinear equations can be reduced to two by eliminating λ; this system
can then be solved by numerical methods, but the existence and unambiguity of solutions has to be ensured by an appropriate choice of the eye point A (see [Kla80],
[KK88]). Figure 4.5 shows a reflection line pattern on a part of a hair dryer and
visualizes some surface irregularities.

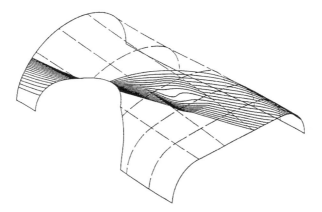

Figure 4.5   Reflection line analysis of a hair dryer.

4.3.2.2   Highlight Lines

The highlight line method also detects surface irregularities and tangent discontinuities
by visualizing special light reflections on the surface. In comparison with the reflection
line method, the highlight lines are calculated independently from any observer's viewpoint.

A highlight line is defined as the loci of all points on the surface where the distance
between the surface normal and the light line is zero. The linear light source idealized
by a straight line with an infinite extension

$$L(t) = L_0 + Bt$$

(A is a point on L, B is a vector defining the direction of L, $t \in \mathbb{R}$) is positioned
above the surface under consideration. For a given surface point $X(u, w)$ let $N(u, w)$
be the unit normal vector. The surface point $X(u, w)$ belongs to the highlight line if

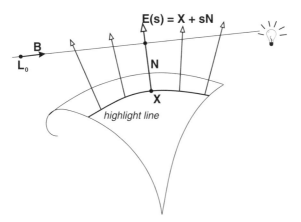

Figure 4.6   Highlight line model.

both lines, $L(t)$ and the extended surface normal

$$E(s) = X(u, w) + s \cdot N(u, w), \quad s \in \mathbb{R}$$

intersect, i.e. if the perpendicular distance

$$d = \frac{\|[B \times N] \cdot [L_0 - X]\|}{\|[B \times N]\|} \tag{4.13}$$

between both lines is zero, see Figure 4.6.

This method can be extended to highlight bands, lines where $d \leq r$ (r fixed) are verified. For details on the algorithms to compute highlight lines, see [BC94].

4.3.2.3   Isophotes

Classical Isophotes: This method analyzes surfaces by lines of equal light intensity, the isophotes. If $X(u, w)$ is a parameterization of the surface and L the direction of a parallel lighting, then the isophote condition is given by:

$$N(u, w) \cdot L = c \tag{4.14}$$

where $c \in \mathbb{R}$ is fixed, see Figure 4.7. Note that silhouettes are special isophotes ($c = 0$) with respect to the light source.

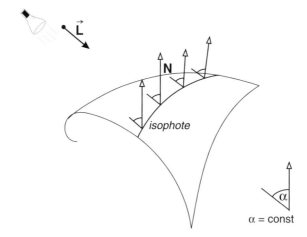

Figure 4.7   Isophote method.

In the same sense as reflection lines and highlight lines, the isophotes provide a powerful tool for visualizing small surface irregularities, which can't be seen with a simple wire frame or a shaded surface image. In Figure 4.8 we use ten different values for c in order to get an isophote pattern on a test surface (left image). Figure 4.8 (middle and right) then differ in the choice of the light direction L.

Now, as stated in the introduction of this section, the light reflection methods can be used to visualize first- and second-order discontinuities, because the surface normal

Figure 4.8   Test surface (left); analysis with isophotes (middle, right).

vector is always involved in the line definitions. We will illustrate this property by using isophotes, for which the following statement holds: *If the surface is C^r-continuous, then the isophotes are C^{r-1}-continuous curves* (for more details see [Poe84]). Figure 4.9 (left) and Figure 4.10 (left) show surfaces displayed as curve networks which don't seem to have discontinuities across the boundaries of their patches. The isophotes on the other hand are discontinuous (gaps) at points where the surface is only C^0 across the boundary of the two patches.

A curvature discontinuity can be recognized, where the isophotes possess tangent discontinuities (breaks). Isophotes are constructed with the isophote conditions,

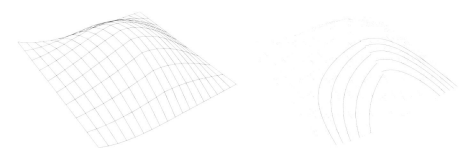

Figure 4.9 C^0-continuous surface, left; analysis with isophotes, right.

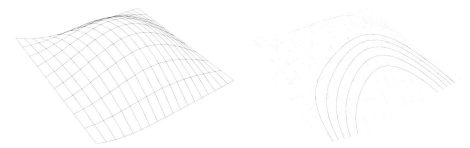

Figure 4.10 C^1-continuous surface, left; analysis with isophotes, right.

whereby in general various different values for c are tested. The equations of type (4.14) are solved numerically.

One should nevertheless be careful when using isophotes for this purpose, because sometimes the breakpoints of the isophotes at curvature discontinuities may not be clearly recognized, because of an ill conditioned light direction. This is the case in Figure 4.10 (right). Either the surface must be rotated, or the light direction must be changed. This special case occurs if the orthogonal projection of the light direction L in the tangent plane at a boundary point $X(u, w)$ is parallel to the tangent of the isophote at this point.

Isophotes for curvature discontinuity: There is another isophote method, which on one hand is an automatic method (independent of a special light direction), but which on the other hand only visualizes curvature discontinuities across the boundaries of a patch work. We give a short description of this algorithm, for the necessary fundamentals of differential geometry, see Section 4.2.

The envelope of the tangent planes along a surface-curve y is a developable, ruled surface Φ. At each point p of y, the tangent $\dot{y}$ is a conjugate to the corresponding ruling of Φ. Conjugate directions are conjugate diameters of the Dupin indicatrix. Such conjugate directions satisfy the symmetric bilinear equation:

$$h_{11}\Delta u \Delta \tilde{u} + h_{12}(\Delta u \Delta \tilde{w} + \Delta \tilde{u} \Delta w) + h_{22} \Delta w \Delta \tilde{w} = 0$$

This relation degenerates at parabolic points, because the asymptotic direction (the direction in which the normal section curvature vanishes) is the conjugate to itself, but also conjugate to all other directions. At planar points, we have this degeneration for each (tangent) direction. Let X_1 and X_2 denote the two G^2 surface patches of the patchwork X, G^1-continuously linked together along the common G^2 boundary curve y. Since both X_1 and X_2 have y as a surface curve, and the tangent planes along y are unique, the Dupin indicatrices i_1, i_2 have a common diameter, but in general there are no further common elements.

We now consider an isophote c passing through P. The tangent t_i of c at P with respect to X_i is conjugate to the orthogonal projection f of the light ray onto the tangent plane ($i = 1, 2$), see Figure 4.11. In general the isophote c shows a tangent discontinuity at P if the Dupin indicatrices of X_1 and X_2 are not equal, but we have to avoid the situations $f = \dot{y} = t$ and $f = t'$. These considerations lead to the following algorithm for displaying the curvature situation across the boundary curves of a patchwork surface:

1. step: give f
2. step: calculate the conjugate directions t_1 and t_2
          and the angle α between t_1 and t_2
3. step: vary $f(\Delta u = \cos \varphi; \Delta w = \sin \varphi)$
          and calculate $\alpha_{\max}$
4. step: **if** $\alpha_{\max} = \pi$
              then the surface is G^2-continuous
              else display curvature discontinuity

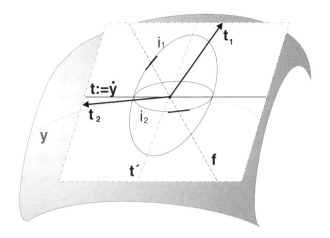

Figure 4.11   Generalized isophote method.

More details about this algorithm can be found in [Pot89]. Figure 4.12 shows the result for G^1- and G^2-continuous surfaces.

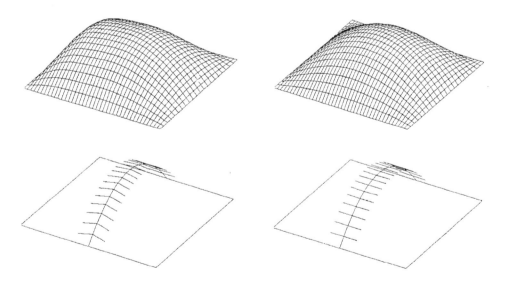

Figure 4.12 G^1-continuous surface, left; G^2-continuous surface, right.

4.3.3   Variable Surface Offsets

Surface curvature is of central importance for surface design. Often the result must be mathematically smooth (continuous in the 2nd derivative) and aesthetically pleasing, i.e., have smooth flowing highlights and shadows. To obtain an aesthetically pleasing shape, the designer works with the curvature. A color map (see Section 4.3.5) can be used to visualize curvature (Gaussian, principal curvatures) over the surface. The problem is the proper choice of the color scale, which depends on the curvature function and therefore on the underlying surface.

The surface interrogation methods presented in this section are therefore *curvature analysis* tools which are able to detect all surface imperfections related to curvature, such as bumps, curvature discontinuity, convexity, and so on.

4.3.3.1   Hedgehog Diagrams and Curvature Plots

The hedgehog diagrams and curvature plots are well known interrogation tools for planar curves (see, for example, [Bei87] and [FS89]). A hedgehog diagram for planar curves visualizes the curve normals proportional to the curvature value at some curve points. A bew curve is obtained by $\tilde{X}_{hedgehog}(t) = X(t) + \kappa N(t)$.

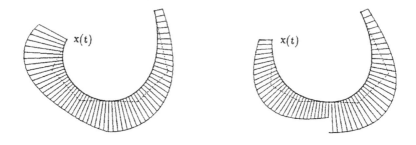

Figure 4.13   Hedgehog diagram for planar curves.

The inspection of surfaces with these methods can be done by applying them to planar curves on the surface (intersections of the surface with planes). Kjellander [Kje83] shows an example of their application.

Hedgehog diagrams for entire surfaces are difficult to interpret and are therefore not to be recommended.

4.3.3.2   Generalized Focal Surfaces

The idea of generalized focal surfaces is quite related to hedgehog diagrams. Instead of drawing surface normals proportional to a function value, only the point on the surface normal proportional to the function is drawn. The loci of all these points is the *generalized focal surface*. This method was introduced by Hagen and Hahmann ([HH92, HHS95]), and is based on the concept of focal surfaces which are known

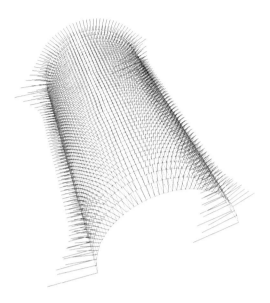

Figure 4.14   Hedgehog diagram for surfaces.

from line geometry. The focal surfaces are the loci of all focal points of a special line congruence, the normal congruence.

Given a set of unit vectors $E(u, w)$ one defines a *line congruence*:

$$C(u, w) = X(u, w) + D(u, w)E(u, w)$$

where $D(u, w)$ is called the signed distance between $X(u, w)$ and $E(u, w)$. If $E(u, w) = N(u, w)$, then C is a normal congruence. A *focal surface* $C_F(u, w)$ is a special normal congruence with $D(u, w) = \kappa_1^{-1}(u, w)$ or $D(u, w) = \kappa_2^{-1}(u, w)$:

$$C_F(u, w) = X(u, w) + \kappa_i^{-1}(u, w)N(u, w) \, , \, i = 1, 2$$

The generalization of this classical concept leads to the *generalized focal surfaces*:

$$F(u, w) = X(u, w) + s\, f(\kappa_1, \kappa_2)\, N(u, w) \, , \quad \text{with} \quad s \in \mathbb{R} \tag{4.15}$$

where N is the unit normal vector of the surface X. f is a real valued function in the parameter values (u, w), see Figure 4.15.

The factor function f can be any arbitrary scalar function, but in the context of surface interrogation it is recommended to take f as a function dependent on the principal curvatures κ_1, κ_2 of X.

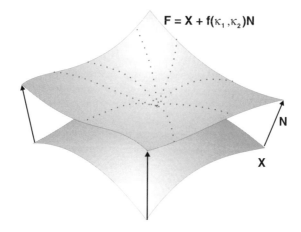

$$\mathbf{F} = \mathbf{X} + \mathbf{f}(\kappa_1, \kappa_2)\mathbf{N}$$

Figure 4.15   Generalized focal surface construction.

variable offset functions:

- $f = \kappa_1 \kappa_2$ Gaussian curvature
- $f = 1/2(\kappa_1 + \kappa_2)$ mean curvature
- $f = (\kappa_1^2 + \kappa_2^2)$ energy functional
- $f = |\kappa_1| + |\kappa_2|$ absolute curvature
- $f = \kappa_i$ principal curvatures
- $f = \frac{1}{\kappa_i}$ focal points
- $f = const$ offset surfaces

Independent of the special choice of the offset function, the generalized focal surfaces F have the following properties:

- second-order surface interrogation method: $X \in C^n \;\; \Rightarrow \;\; F \in C^{n-2}$
- pinpoint property
- zoom property: s allows to zoom in or out a surface region of interest
- fast computation: pointwise evaluation of second- and third-order derivatives.

The different offset functions listed below can now be used to interrogate and visualize surfaces with respect to the following criteria:

- convexity test
- detection of flat points
- detection of surface irregularities
- visualization of curvature behaviour
- visualization of technical smoothness
- visualization of C^2- and C^3-discontinuities
- test of technical aspects

Examples of application:

- It is the only method which is able to detect *flat points*. A flat point is a special umbilic point, with $\kappa_1 = \kappa_2 = 0$. These are undesired surface points because they

make the surface bumpy. The detection of flat points can be done by choosing one
of the offset functions:

$$f = |\kappa_1| + |\kappa_2| \qquad (4.16)$$
$$f = \kappa_1^2 + \kappa_2^2 \qquad (4.17)$$

A flat point occurs where both surfaces touch.

- **convexity test:** A surface is locally convex at $X(u, w)$, if the Gaussian curvature
is positive at this point. Often a surface is called non convex, if there is a change
in the sign of the Gaussian curvature. If one takes the offset function

$$f = \kappa_1 \cdot \kappa_2 = K \qquad (4.18)$$

the two surfaces $X(u, w)$ and $F(u, w)$ intersect at the parabolic points. An example
is shown in Figure 4.16. The generalized focal surface therefore pinpoints directly
on the area where the sign of K changes.

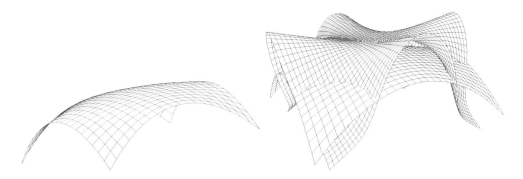

Figure 4.16   Convexity test with generalized focal surfaces.

Orthotomics (see Section 4.3.4.1), which are also used to test the convexity, don't
pin-point on the surface area where the problem arrives. Generalized focal surfaces
not only visualize surface imperfections, they also give the user a 3D impression of the
relative amount of the offset function over the surface, which color maps can't do.

- **mathematical smoothness:** By using the offset function

$$f = \kappa_1^2 + \kappa_2^2 , \qquad (4.19)$$

the discontinuities of the second or third derivatives can be visualized by the generalized focal surfaces which are only C^{-1} or C^0 there (see Figure 4.17).
- **visualizing technical aspects:** A surface which should be treated by a spherical
cutter is not allowed to have a curvature radius smaller than the radius of the cutter
R_{cutter}. The generalized focal surfaces are able to detect such undesired regions by

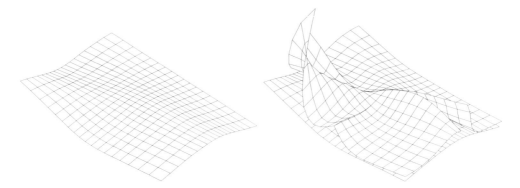

Figure 4.17   4 bicubic patches: curvature discontinuity.

intersection with the surface X. The offset function to choose in this special case, is

$$f = \frac{1}{R_{cutter}} - \kappa_{max} \qquad (4.20)$$

Figure 4.18 shows such a surface which is not allowed to be cut.

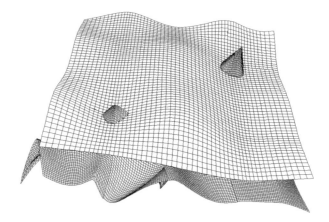

Figure 4.18   Milling test.

- **visualizing surface irregularities:** Surfaces are aesthetically pleasing if they have "nice" light reflections. The reflection line methods visualize this property. The generalized focal surfaces are also a tool for visualizing such surface imperfections because they are very sensitive to small irregularities in the shape. In Figure 4.19 parts of a hair dryer are shown. They consist of biquintic C^1-continuous patches. The isoparametric lines don't reflect the bump in the surface, which is however emphasized by the focal analysis on the bottom right.

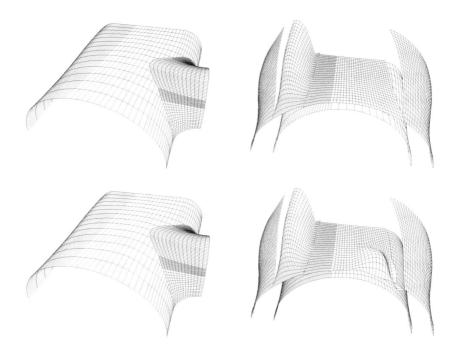

Figure 4.19   Hair dryer: fairness test with generalized focal surfaces.

4.3.4   Detection of Inflections

The polarity method and the orthotomics are both interactive interrogation tools, which only detect one surface "imperfection": the change of the sign in the Gaussian curvature. Surfaces with only convex isoparameter lines are not necessarily convex in the sense that their Gaussian curvature need not be positive at all surface points. Such surface imperfections can not always be seen and need a special analysis: color maps, generalized focal surfaces or the following two methods can do this.

4.3.4.1   Orthotomics

If we start with a surface $X(u, w)$ and a point P, which is not on X and which does not lie on any tangent plane of X, P is reflected by a tangent plane of X and we multiply this length by a factor k. The parameter form of the k-orthotomic surface of X with respect to P is

$$Y_k(u, w) = P + k\Big((X(u, w) - P) \cdot N(u, w)\Big) N(u, w), \qquad (4.21)$$

where $N(u, w)$ is the unit normal vector of the surface.

The following is important for applications [Hos84]:

Let $X(u, w)$ be a regular surface and let P be a point not on the surface or on any tangential plane of the surface. The k-orthotomic surface $Y_k(u, w)$ of $X(u, w)$ with respect to P has a singularity in (u_0, w_0), if and only if the Gaussian curvature of X vanishes, or changes its sign at this point.

Figure 4.20   Bicubic surface patch, left; orthotomic analysis, right.

To illustrate this method we consider a Bézier surface with completely convex parameter lines, shown in Figure 4.20, left. But this surface is not convex: as Figure 4.20, right, shows, the orthotomic analysis emphasizes the change of sign of the Gaussian curvature in the corner region.

4.3.4.2   Polarity Method

The polarity method is an interactive method able to detect unwanted changes in the sign of the Gaussian curvature. For curves it detects inflection points. It uses the polar image of a curve or surface, where the singularities (cusps, edge of regression) of this image indicate the existence of points with vanishing Gaussian curvature.

We will describe the principle of this method using a planar curve $X(t) = (x(t), y(t))$. An arbitrary point (parameter $t = t_0$) on this curve is mapped by the polarity at the unit circle onto the straight line $x(t_0) + \eta y(t_0) + 1 = 0$. If t is varied within its definition range, the created set of straight lines envelope a polar curve $P(t)$ of $X(t)$. Differentiation and elimination lead to the parameter form of $P(t)$:

$$P(t) = \begin{bmatrix} \xi(t) \\ \eta(t) \end{bmatrix} = \begin{bmatrix} \dfrac{-\dot{y}}{x\dot{y} - \dot{x}y}, \dfrac{\dot{x}}{x\dot{y} - \dot{x}y} \end{bmatrix}^T \tag{4.22}$$

The polar curve of a curve in 3D is determined in an analogue way.

In the case of a surface in parameter form $X(u, w) = (x(u, w), y(u, w), z(u, w))$, the result of a polarity at the unit sphere is a polar surface $P(u, w)$ with the parameter form:

$$P(u, w) = N \cdot \frac{\det|N, X_1, X_2|}{\det|X, X_1, X_2|} = \frac{[X_2 \times X_1]}{\det|X, X_1, X_2|}. \tag{4.23}$$

The following facts are important for applications:

- If the planar curve $X(t)$ has an inflection point for $t = t_0$, then the polar curve $P(t)$ has a singularity for $t = t_0$.
- If the surface $X(u, w)$ has a root or change of sign in the Gaussian curvature at (u_0, w_0), then the polar surface has a singularity here.

The polar surface in Figure 4.21 looks similar to the orthotomic surface in Figure 4.20, because the center of polarity is chosen to be equal with the projection point of the orthotomic analysis (see Section 4.3.4.1). For more informations about the polarity method and how to remove the inflections, see [Hos85].

4.3.5   Color Mappings

While displaying a shaded image of the surface one is free to choose a color for each surface point. *Color maps* are used to visualize functions over a surface and *texturing* can emphasize the spatial perception of a 2D image of the surface.

4.3.5.1   Color Maps

A color-coded map is an application, which associates to a scalar function value a specific color. The color scale presents an even gradation of color corresponding to the range of function values. Colors are principally used to visualize either continuously or discontinuously any scalar function over a surface (see, for example [Dil81], [BFFH88], [For79]), such as pressure, temperature, or curvature. Colors are used as a fourth dimension and show the user immediately and quantitatively how the function varies over the surface.

The Gaussian curvature map conveys information about local surface shape. It displays unwanted local behaviors as well as surface irregularities, because it is very sensitive to small changes of the Gaussian curvature, if the color is well encoded.

An even gradation of the linear or cyclic color-coding is important in visualizing the rapid curvature variation by the presence of color fringes. Beck, et al. [BFH86] propose using the HSI (hue, saturation, intensity) model and performing transformations between this space and the three primary colors RGB. See [FvDFH90] for more details on color spaces and transformations.

An example of discrete color-coding of the interval [0,1] is the following one:

Figure 4.21   Polar surface of a bicubic Bézier patch.

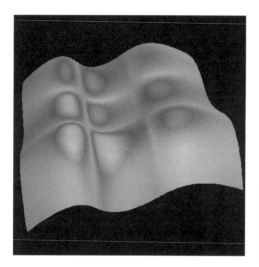 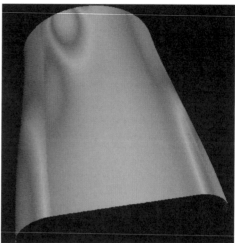

Figure 4.22   Color codings of Gaussian curvature. (See also color Plate 13)

interval	Red	Green	Blue	Color
0.0 - 0.2	1	0	0	red
0.2 - 0.4	1	1	0	yellow
0.4 - 0.6	0	1	0	green
0.6 - 0.8	0	1	1	turquoise
0.8 - 1.0	0	0	1	blue

If one is interested in the change of sign of the Gaussian curvature K for a convexity test, one might assign the color red to areas with positive Gaussian curvature, areas where K is negative are blue, and areas where it is near zero are yellow. Color maps of the maximum and minimum principal curvatures are of primary interest when a surface is to be machined by a spherical cutter (see also Section 4.3.3.2).

The main difficulty in this simple interrogation method is the choice of a convenient color scale, which obviously is dependent on the function values to be visualized.

4.3.5.2   Pseudo Texture

The use of colors for displaying a surface helps to emphasize the 3D understanding of a 2D image by simulating the shadows, perspective and depth of the object. An artificial texturing is an aid for visualizing rendered surfaces. Isoparametric lines are commonly used, but they are in some situations ambiguous. Schweitzer [Sch83] projects equally spaced dots of equal size over the surface in order to increase the visual perception of the form.

4.3.6   Characteristic Lines

In this section two methods for analyzing surfaces are presented: *lines of curvature* and *geodesic paths*. In each case a net of lines on the surface can be created, and should be interpreted with the knowledge of differential geometry. These are the most sophisticated tools from the mathematician's point of view. The use of these tools is nevertheless limited, because of their cumbersome calculations and the lack of intuition in interpretation of their pattern. From the practical point of view, users should be used to interpreting the lines of curvature or the geodesic paths, otherwise they won't have any profit. Numerous graphical examples are illustrated in [Por94] and [Far87].

4.3.6.1   Lines of Curvature, Umbilics

Lines of curvature are curves whose tangent directions coincide with those of the principal directions, which are orthogonal. They form therefore an orthogonal net on the surface.

The net of lines of curvature becomes singular at an umbilical point where κ_1 and κ_2 are identical and the principal directions are indeterminate. Some numerical integration method is used to calculate the lines of curvature. But the integration process becomes unstable near an umbilic. Unfortunately umbilics appear frequently on free form surfaces. Recent work on umbilics [MWP96], destined for use in CAGD[2], presents a procedure for computing the lines of curvature near an umbilic. And in [MP94] a computational method for locating all isolated umbilics on parametric polynomial surfaces is described. However, umbilics and lines of curvature figure can be studied in classical differential geometry literature, like [Dar96], or in a more recent book of Porteous [Por94]. We don't want to extend this aspect here and shall now focus on the computation of lines of curvature.

Every principal curvature direction vector must fulfill equation (4.7). Solving the first equation of (4.7) we get

$$\dot{u} = \frac{du}{ds} = \alpha(h_{12} + \kappa g_{12})$$

$$\dot{w} = \frac{dw}{ds} = -\alpha(h_{11} + \kappa g_{11}) \tag{4.24}$$

where α is an arbitrary nonzero factor. Since the principal direction vector must also satisfy the second equation of (4.7), we get

$$\dot{u} = \frac{du}{ds} = \beta(h_{22} + \kappa g_{22})$$

$$\dot{w} = \frac{dw}{ds} = -\beta(h_{12} + \kappa g_{12}) \tag{4.25}$$

The solutions $\dot{u}$ and $\dot{w}$ of (4.24) and (4.25) are linearly dependent, because the system of linear equations given by (4.7) has rank less than 2.

---

[2] CAGD: Computer Aided Geometric Design

It remains to calculate α and β. We eliminate these factors by adopting arc-length s to parameterize the curvature line and by using the normalization condition

$$g_{11}\left(\frac{du}{ds}\right)^2 + 2g_{12}\left(\frac{du}{ds}\right)\left(\frac{dw}{ds}\right) + g_{22}\left(\frac{dw}{ds}\right)^2 = 1. \tag{4.26}$$

Substituting (4.24) and (4.25) respectively into (4.26) gives the factors

$$\alpha = \frac{\pm 1}{\sqrt{g_{11}(h_{12}+\kappa g_{12})^2 - 2g_{12}(h_{12}+\kappa g_{12})(h_{11}+\kappa g_{11}) + g_{22}(h_{11}+\kappa g_{11})^2}}$$

$$\beta = \frac{\pm 1}{\sqrt{g_{11}(h_{22}+\kappa g_{22})^2 - 2g_{12}(h_{22}+\kappa g_{22})(h_{12}+\kappa g_{12}) + g_{22}(h_{12}+\kappa g_{12})^2}},$$

where κ represents either of the two principal curvatures κ_1, κ_2.

To solve these two coupled, nonlinear differential equations (4.24) or alternatively (4.25) (the solutions obtained from (4.24) and (4.25) are linearly dependent), a numerical integration method for initial value problems must be used: a constant-step fourth-order *Runge-Kutta method* or multi-step *predictor-corrector methods*, like Adams methods [Str86]. The initial conditions are the coordinates (u, w) of a starting point, since at each point the lines of curvature are unique.

Some practical hints for using such a method when integrating across a multipatch surface are given in [BFH86]. Maekawa, et al. [MWP96] explain in more detail the appropriate choice of the sign of α and β. They also point out that in some special situations it is preferable to solve either equation (4.24) or (4.25).

4.3.6.2   Geodesic Paths

Geodesic paths are lines which connect two points on a curved surface with minimum path length. A lot of practical applications related to optimal path finding make use of geodesic paths, for example optimal motion planning on a curved surface for robot programming. The study of geodesics is a rather complex concern and needs a lot more theoretical and numerical attention than the following overview can provide (for a rigorous treatment of geodesics see for example [Kre59] and [Eis76]).

A general parametric curve (path) $C = C(t) = (u(t), w(t))$ on the surface X is given by $\bar{X}(t) = X(u(t), w(t))$. The length of this surface path between two points with parameter values t_0 and t_1 is then obtained by integration of the line element (called distance element) (4.3)

$$s = \int_{t_0}^{t_1} \sqrt{\dot{\bar{X}}^2}\, dt = \int_{t_0}^{t_1} \sqrt{g_{11}\dot{u}^2 + 2g_{12}\dot{u}\dot{w} + g_{22}\dot{w}^2}\, dt \tag{4.27}$$

We now introduce a perturbation of this path by

$$\begin{aligned}
\tilde{u}(t) &= u(t) + \varepsilon p(t) \\
\tilde{w}(t) &= w(t) + \varepsilon q(t)
\end{aligned} \tag{4.28}$$

where ε is a small parameter, and we are interested in the change in s. p and q must satisfy the end conditions $p(0) = p(1) = q(0) = q(1) = 0$. We need to find at the end the path which causes the distance to attain extreme values. To do so we substitute the path (4.28) in equation (4.27) and keep only the terms which are of first order in ε. Setting then $ds/d\varepsilon = 0$ for extreme path length, we get the Euler equations:

$$\frac{d}{dt}\frac{\partial\Phi}{\partial\dot{u}} - \frac{\partial\Phi}{\partial u} = 0$$

$$\frac{d}{dt}\frac{\partial\Phi}{\partial\dot{w}} - \frac{\partial\Phi}{\partial w} = 0$$

where $\Phi(u, w, \dot{u}, \dot{w}) = \sqrt{g_{11}\dot{u}^2 + 2g_{12}\dot{u}\dot{w} + g_{22}\dot{w}^2}dt$. These are the *geodesic differential equations*, which have to be satisfied by geodesic paths.

To bring them in a more convenient form for numerical computations, one chooses arc-length s for the parameter variable t and gets by use of equation (4.3) the following equations:

$$\frac{d^2u}{ds^2} + \Gamma_{11}^1\left(\frac{du}{ds}\right)^2 + 2\Gamma_{12}^1\left(\frac{du}{ds}\right)\left(\frac{dw}{ds}\right) + \Gamma_{22}^1\left(\frac{dw}{ds}\right)^2 = 0$$

$$\frac{d^2w}{ds^2} + \Gamma_{11}^2\left(\frac{du}{ds}\right)^2 + 2\Gamma_{12}^2\left(\frac{du}{ds}\right)\left(\frac{dw}{ds}\right) + \Gamma_{22}^2\left(\frac{dw}{ds}\right)^2 = 0$$

(4.29)

where Γ_{ij}^k (i,j,k = 1,2) are the *Christoffel symbols* of second kind:

$$\Gamma_{ij}^1 = \frac{N \cdot [X_{ij} \times X_2]}{\|[X_1 \times X_2]\|}, \qquad \Gamma_{ij}^2 = \frac{N \cdot [X_1 \times X_{ij}]}{\|[X_1 \times X_2]\|}$$

A curve on the surface $X(u, w)$, which satisfies these two second-order differential equations, is a geodesic. A geodesic path is uniquely determined by a starting point (u, w) and a direction $(du/ds, dw/ds)$ satisfying equation (4.26).

For numerical purposes it is recommended to transform equation (4.29) into four first order equations in four variables (u, w, u', w'):

$$\frac{du}{ds} = u'$$

$$\frac{dw}{ds} = w'$$

(4.30)

$$\frac{du'}{ds} = -\Gamma_{11}^1 u'^2 - 2\Gamma_{12}^1 u'w' - \Gamma_{22}^1 w'^2$$

$$\frac{dw'}{ds} = -\Gamma_{11}^2 u'^2 - 2\Gamma_{12}^2 u'w' - \Gamma_{22}^2 w'^2 .$$

An appropriate Runge-Kutta method can be applied for numerical integration. The algorithm provides a method for performing initial value integrations of geodesic paths, i.e., an initial value and a start direction must be given. It is numerically more difficult to perform boundary-value integration, i.e., the specification of geodesic paths between two given points on the surface. A solution for that problem can be found in [Far87].

5

Vector Field Visualization Techniques

Roger Crawfis
The Ohio State University

Nelson Max
Lawrence Livermore National Laboratory

ABSTRACT

Many techniques for 3D vector field visualization have been developed over the past several years, with a recent flurry of activity. All of the techniques outlined below can be placed under one of three themes – particle advection, texture generation, or classification/representation techniques. This chapter will give an (noncomprehensive) overview of current techniques and recent research algorithms for representing flow fields.

5.1 PARTICLE ADVECTION TECHNIQUES

Experimental fluid dynamicists use a variety of techniques to examine flow fields. Hydrogen bubbles or pH dyes can be injected into a fluid and photographed. Smoke can be introduced into an airflow and observed. The references in [Yan94] contain several other techniques that have been developed over the years. Most of these rely on injecting a foreign substance into the flow and observing the effects the flow field has on this substance. Advection is the local change of this foreign substance caused by the flow field, or the transport of this foreign substance due to the flow field. The techniques outlined in this section follow this theme of injecting a (virtual) foreign substance into the flow field and visualizing it.

Data Visualization Techniques, Edited by C. Bajaj

5.1.1 Individual Particles and Streamlines

By releasing and advecting abstract weightless particles in a flow field, we can simulate a variety of effects. The particles can be represented as raster points in the simplest of schemes. As these particles are advected, their raster positions are updated and the motion of the particle can be studied. Just using raster points can lead to clutter and a meaningless image when many particles are displayed simultaneously. Reeves [RB85, Ree83] introduced structured particle systems for representing fuzzy objects. These were applied to image synthesis to produce fuzzy phenomena such as grass, trees, fire and waterfalls. Sims [Sim90] developed a parallel system for handling particles with hidden surfaces and anti-aliasing and applied these to a two-dimensional vector field; van Wijk [vW93a, vW92] uses a particle system with shading and motion blurring of the particles to represent a flow field. Depth of field and hidden particle removal are added to aid in the comprehension of the flow. Max, et al. [MCG94] render particles passing around or through a contour surface to show the relationship between the surface and the flow. Particles fade in as they approach the surface and fade out as they leave it. Particles are also given a lifetime, with new particles generated as time progresses. A small texture mapped square is stretched in the direction of the projected flow and composited into the image. A texture image of a smooth dot is used for both the intensity and the opacity, hence only motion blurred particles are rendered. See Chapter 6, Section 6.4.2 in this volume.

For steady-state flows or a single time-step, we can connect a particle's current position to the position it would be advected to for a constant flow. Repeating for several time-steps and accumulating the line segments yields a streamline. This is one of the most popular techniques, due to its simplicity and reliance on only a single time-step's worth of data. The streamline has the property that it is everywhere tangential to the flow field. Suppose we apply the same technique to an unsteady flow, where the velocity changes as a function of time. By connecting the positions of a single moving particle at successive time steps, we get what is called a pathline. For a steady flow, this will be the same as a streamline, but in an unsteady flow, the pathline will depend on the instant of time at which the particle was released.

Now suppose a visible foreign substance is continuously realesed into an unsteady flow from a fixed position. It will produce a streak, or streakline. This can be approximated computationally by creating a new particle at the release point for each time-step, and tracking all released particles by advecting them according to their current velocities. The current positions of all the particles are connected by line segments, in the order of their release times, in order to approximate the streakline. For steady flows, streaklines are also the same as streamlines. Figure 5.1 illustrates the differences between streamlines, streaklines and pathlines for unsteady flow fields. Plate 14 (see color plate section) illustrates the effect possible with a large number of streamlines on a Harrier jet simulation (image courtesy of Vee Hirsch, NASA Ames). Finally, timelines are a tool for observing the velocity magnitude and gradient of a flow. Rather than connecting particles originating from the same position at different times, a line of particles is injected into the flow at a single time. This is similar to a string blowing in the wind, where the shape gives an indicator of the flow history.

Hin and Post [HP93] use particles with random walks to simulate the dispersion within a field. Particles are released normally as above, but for the advection, a slight

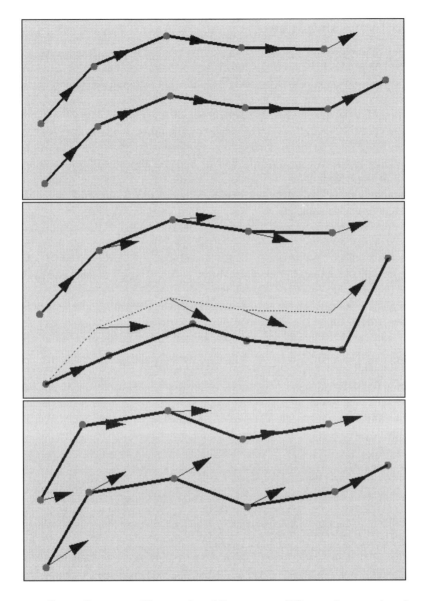

Figure 5.1 Streamlines, streaklines and pathlines at two different time or advection steps.

random perturbation or inaccuracy is introduced. Comparing the random walk streamlines to the traditional streamline represents the divergence from the original streamline. Several such random walk streamlines need to be positioned around the starting
location of the original streamline.

5.1.2   Ribbons and Tubes

If we have two streamlines starting from nearby points, we can draw line segments between those points and between their subsequent advected positions. This will yield a surface that can be rendered. Two starting points in a flow may diverge substantially from each other. Experimental techniques used to understand flows typically use a small ribbon that is assumed to be weightless with regard to the flow. Constructing a ribbon from two streamlines – the edges of the ribbon – will not work, since the streamlines may diverge from each other. A ribbon for scientific visualization purposes therefore needs to preserve its width. Several algorithms for constraining the divergence of the ribbon edges are possible. Three streamlines can be used, such that a middle one controls the advected length, and the direction that the ribbon twists about is calculated from the streamlines a delta on either side. New starting points for the outer streamlines are used at the edge of the ribbon for each sequential advection calculation. A ribbon illustrates not only the direction of the flow, but also its curl by the amount of twisting in the ribbon. Pagendarm and Walter [PW94] describe an algorithm for constructing the stream ribbon using a single streamline and the curl calculated numerically from the flow field.

We can also calculate a circle a delta away from the streamline that is perpendicular to the flow. Advecting this circle will result in a streamline rendered as a cylindrical tube. The radius of the circle can be constrained in a similar manner as the stream ribbons, or it can be allowed to grow and become elliptical. Schroeder [SVL91] uses a regular polygon rather than a circle to show the local strain or strain-rate that the streamline passes through. He also shows how several scalar variables can be mapped onto this construct which he calls a stream polygon. The color of each edge of the regular polygon can represent a different variable as can the overall radius of the stream polygon.

5.1.3   Stream Surfaces

A stream surface [Hul92] extends the concept of a ribbon by allowing adjacent streamlines to diverge. A triangular mesh is created between the streamlines. As the streamlines diverge, more streamlines are added and a finer triangulation is generated. Streamlines are merged in areas of stagnation. The stream surface is thus everywhere tangent to the flow field (with fine enough accuracy in the subdivision). This is useful for showing the containment of a flow, that is, the boundary that a flow will not cross. Kenwright and Mallinson [KM92] present an accurate construction of stream surfaces incrementally using dual stream functions. van Wijk [vW93b] gives an algorithm for constructing stream surfaces implicitly by generating a volume density that can be isocontoured. Ma and Smith [MS93] study the mixing and dispersion of convection–diffusion problems, by taking a streamline and allowing it not only to propagate forward, but also to disperse by incremental standard deviations. Consecutive circular contours are then connected to form a surface for rendering. The resulting tubes can intersect each other illustrating areas of high mixing.

5.1.4   Flow Volumes

Max, et al. [MBC93, MCW93] extend the notion of stream surfaces to a flow volume. A seed polygon which acts as a smoke generator is placed into the flow field under user control. This is a natural technique that is closely related to experimental techniques that release smoke or dye into a flow field. As the vector field passes through the polygon, smoke is propagated forward, sweeping out a volume which is subdivided into tetrahedra. Compression and expansion of the volume due to the flow can be taken into account by adjusting the opacity based on the tetrahedron's volume. As the flow volume expands, they employ an adaptive mesh refinement technique to ensure the curvature of the resulting volume is accurate. Figure 5.2 illustrates a sampling volume and mesh generated using this technique. The complex topology of the flow volume would require a general sorting method to yield a valid back-to-front sort in order to apply a volume rendering technique. However, for this application, the smoke or dye can be a constant color throughout the volume. They show that the resulting integration of the volume density is independent of the order in which the volume cells are processed for constant colored volume cells. Thus, no sorting is required for constant colored smoke. They are able to achieve real-time interaction by rendering the smoke, rather than an entire volume, using graphics hardware for the rendering, as described in Chapter 6 of this book, Section 6.3.2. They also add additional features that allow the user to watch moving puffs of smoke, control the time propagation of the smoke, and combine opaque geometry with the smoke. A general polyhedra sort [SBM94] can be added and the smoke can be colored by a separate scalar variable. The flow through a HEPA filter (High-Efficiency Particulant Absorption filter) is probed with a flow volume in Plate 15 (see color plate section).

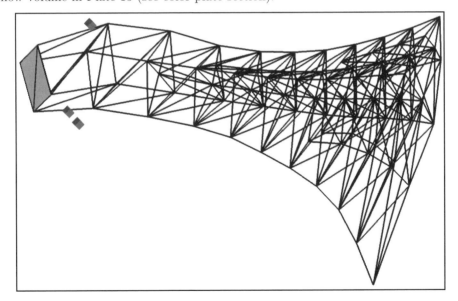

Figure 5.2   A mesh generated using the flow volumes technique.

5.1.5   Streamballs

Metaballs [Nea95], blobbies [KV90], or soft-objects [Mit87] are flexible algorithms for modeling fuzzy phenomena. A density volume is created by placing generating points in the volume's space. A basis function is centered at each of these points, contributing to the overall density function throughout the space. Gaussian functions are usually used, centered at each generating point. A continuous function is thus created with the value at any point in space as the sum of the point-centered Guassians evaluated at that point. An isocontour surface of the resulting density function can be used to represent objects. Brill, et al. [BHR+94] introduced streamballs that use particles or streamlines as metaball location points. The resulting surfaces split gracefully in areas of high divergence and gracefully join back together in areas of convergence. For large metaballs the results can be misleading since only the centers of the metaballs correspond to the flow path.

5.1.6   Advection Numerics

All of these techniques rely on a procedure to advect a massless particle from one position to another. If we are given the velocity $(\bar{\nu})$ at the particle's current position $(\bar{p})$, then for a differential time dt, the particle's new position will be $\bar{p}' = \bar{p} + dt \cdot \bar{\nu}$. If we desire the particle's position at a time t_1, then an integration of this process is needed to go from the current time to a later time t_1. This is an initial value ODE problem for which an extensive set of literature exists. The simplest solution is the forward or explicit Euler solution:

$$\bar{p}_{n+1} = \bar{p}_n + \Delta t \bar{\nu}_n + O(\Delta t^2)$$

More advanced techniques exist [Hof92, Pea88], of which Fourth-Order Runge-Kutta is the preferred method.

These techniques require ascertaining the vector field at intermediate positions. If the calculation of the vector field at these intermediate points is costly, the overall cost of the advection can grow quickly. Since the vector field is usually defined on a mesh, calculating the vector field at a point interior to a zone requires an interpolation algorithm. Trilinear interpolation is one of the simplest techniques for regular or rectilinear meshes, but may not be very accurate. Higher-order techniques will require more data points. For curvilinear meshes, interpolation can be performed in computational space [?] with a mapping to and from physical space based on the Jacobian. For other mesh types, interpolation with higher-order interpolation methods is quite complex with many end cases (see [KM92] and [USM95]). Time dynamic fields offer the additional complexity of interpolation of a surface in four dimensions [KM92, BLM95, Lan94]. Storage must also be allocated for each time-step needed for the interpolation.

Since two nearby particles in a flow can diverge substantially from each other, care must be taken to ensure accuracy. When many particles are being advected, this cost can be quite high. The storage of the particles plus the storage of the vector field at multiple time-steps is also a disadvantage of advection techniques.

5.2 GLOBAL TECHNIQUES VIA TEXTURE GENERATION

The techniques outlined above all limit the representation of the vector field to the user-selected region, the generation points (points for particles and streamlines; curves for stream surfaces; and polygons for flow volumes), and the volume advected from that region. They offer a more detailed examination of the history of a flow from a particular spot. However, a user trying to get an overall feel for the entire 3D domain would have to move the generation points through the entire volume (or most of it) in order to ensure that all regions of the field were represented. The techniques outlined in this section all try to represent an overview of the entire volume (or large portions of it) by creating a localized pattern of icons. They rely on localized coherence of individual icons to create a seamless texture and hence usually do not require advection. Several experimental techniques follow this theme. Miniature tufts can be scattered throughout a wind tunnel or across the surface of an airfoil. A viscous oil can be spread across a surface, so that when the flow impinges on the surface it scatters the oil into visual patterns. [Yan94] contains several other examples.

5.2.1 Hedgehogs, Tufts or Arrows

Many visualization systems allow you to place at positions within the flow arrows or vectors which are oriented in the direction of the flow. These work fine for slices of the data, but tend to get very cluttered and exhibit bad aliasing artifacts when examining the entire 3D vector field. These techniques do not really attempt to generate a texture or pattern for the flow, but rather present a quantitative icon at each regularly spaced data point. They are included here for completeness. Most of the work below attempts to show the broad overview that hedgehogs give for 2D slices, but in a clearer less cluttered framework. If the textures are smooth enough and avoid clutter, then they can be applied to 3D flows successfully. Section 5.2.2 will go over the Line Bundle technique in detail and present some of the overall goals of the techniques in this section.

5.2.2 Line Bundles

Most workstations offer hardware support for drawing lines while high-end workstations are capable of drawing several million lines per second. Line Bundles capitalize on this to generate very fast representations of a flow field as an anisotropic volume density cloud, or a contour surface with anisotropic reflection.

A line bundle is defined as a collection of line segments all oriented in the same direction and relatively close together. The line segments are placed randomly within a unit cube. A line bundle is then rendered at each (or selected) data point, following the volume rendering technique of splatting, to produce a three-dimensional texture. The term *line bundles* used here has no relationship to the term *line bundles* used in abstract mathematics. Line bundle here refer to exactly that, a tight bundle of lines.

5.2.2.1   Stochastic Textures

The goal of this technique is the generation of a seamless texture throughout space that can represent the flow field. Stochastic texture generation has been studied by several authors for 2D images [CA91, Lew84, Per85]. Three-dimensional texture generation has been explored by only a few authors [CM92b, Lew90, KH89, CL93].

This technique generates textures for flow visualization by drawing many small line segments in a back-to-front order. Drawing these line segments very closely together will fill in the projected image space with a constant color. By using semi-transparent anti-aliased lines and alpha blending, this fill-in will be reduced, but with enough line segments the colors will saturate the device and still fill in the image. Jittering the hue or saturation of the line segments and blending them together allows for a smoother texture. Jittering of the line segments' color is allowed in all three channels of hue, saturation and value space. Plate 16 (see color plate section) uses line bundles to represent the flow near the surface of theoretical Aerogel particles. Aerogel is a new very lightweight material being used for insulation, packaging, filters, cosmetics and many other applications where materials with very low weight and high surface area are needed.

In addition to the overall color of the line segments, the color and opacity of the head and tail of the segments can be modified as follows. The head of the line segment (the end that will point in the vector field direction) is optionally desaturated to give an indicator of the positive direction of the vector field along the line segments. Both the head and the tail of the line segments are made more transparent than the base to allow the line segment to gradually fade into the background. The tail is set to completely fade into the background, while the head is only slightly more transparent than the midpoint. This is similar to a painter gradually lifting his or her brush at the end of a long stroke. Without this blending, harsh edges would be visible at the endpoints and unwanted patterns would appear in the image. These changes to the head and tail of a line segment require at least three points to define them, and hence affect the rendering speed of the overall image. The hardware interpolates the colors along the line segments to produce a gradual change.

The number of lines used is a critical factor in generating a smooth texture. Too few lines do not yield a texture, while too many affect the performance of the rendering and increase the opacity, hiding information behind them. As more lines are added, more of the screen real estate is filled in and an overall texture is generated. A continuous texture will lead to a less distracting view of the vector field. See Plate 16.

The overlap of the lines is also critical to achieving a smooth texture. Two user controls are offered to control the overlap – the overall splat size and a vector scale factor. The splat size needs to be large enough for an overlap of the lines in all directions from the splat data point to fill enough of the image space to create a texture. The vector scale can be used to highlight vectors with greater magnitude or to give a more wispy appearance to the image. It is also required for vector fields that have not been normalized for world coordinates. That is, it is necessary to scale a vector field from its physical space or units to world coordinates.

5.2.2.2   Back-to-front Compositing

To create an unambiguous texture in three dimensions, it is critical that the line bundles are drawn in back-to-front order. The current implementation uses an octree to store the raw data values of interest (i.e., the vector field at discrete points). A back-to-front sorting of this octree is then determined on every redraw. The line bundles are drawn in back-to-front order with a user-specified opacity and then blended into the image. Individual lines are not sorted within a bundle. This sorting and back-to-front compositing closely follows the splatting technique for volume rendering of scalar fields.

Disabling the z-buffering within a bundle allows the line segments to be drawn as if on top of each other to produce the desired texture. This is accomplished by setting the OpenGL z-buffering function to "test but do not set", so that line bundles will not modify the z-buffer, but will examine it and only render to pixels for which the line bundles lie in front. By drawing the line bundles last when other opaque geometry is to be rendered, they are blended into the image appropriately. See Plate 16.

5.2.2.3   Orientation

The line bundle is centered at the splat data point and oriented in the direction of the vector field at that data point. This differs from splatting, where the footprint image (i.e, the splat) must be perpendicular to the viewing direction. For efficiency, the line bundles are precomputed by calculating the color jittering and the relative placement of a set of lines and drawing them into an OpenGL display list. All of the lines for this display list are oriented in the positive z-direction. For each redraw, a translation to the splat center and an orientation to the vector field direction need to be calculated before posting the display list. A rotation matrix is calculated to rotate the z-axis to the vector field direction. The lines are stretched in the z-axis by the vector field magnitude and a user-specified scaling factor before this rotation. The properly oriented line bundle is then translated into the proper position and composited into the image. This translation is slightly jittered to break up possible regular patterns, producing a smoother texture.

5.2.2.4   Color-coding

The line bundles discussed so far produce a rather homogeneous texture. The colors vary locally, but globally the variation is constant. It is useful to represent either the velocity magnitude or another variable using color encoding. Jittering about a different hue for line bundles representing different scalar values allows an anisotropic texture that can be color-coded. Each splat has an associated color assigned to it by the user. When rendering, a new line bundle is created with the line segments' colors jittered using the splat's color as a base color. This differs from the homogeneous line bundles in that there, all of the splats had the same base color. In Plate 17 (see color plate section) the line bundles are applied to the flow through an Aerogel substrate. Small spheres are used to represent areas occupied by Aerogel in the simulation. Plate 17 depicts areas of high velocity magnitude within the Aerogel, where the color represents the velocity magnitude. High velocity magnitudes are represented by magenta, and low velocity magnitudes are represented by yellow.

5.2.2.5 Lighting

Lighting can add an additional depth cue to a visualization. Kajiya [KH89], Hanson [HC93], and Banks [Ban94] have developed algorithms for lighting curves in three-space. These techniques work especially well for opaque curves. For many small and fairly transparent line segments the benefit of lighting is not as great. Furthermore, it may introduce distracting artifacts into the desired texture. Lighting of curves is also not supported in hardware, so the individual colors of each line segment need to be modified. Since different orientations of the line bundles are lighted differently, this prohibits the use of precomputed display lists.

5.2.3 Spot Noise

van Wijk [vW91] created a 2D texture in the direction of the vector field that could be mapped to parametric surfaces. Small spots of varying amplitude and size are randomly deposited onto the 2D plane to produce a texture. Different shapes of the spots produce different patterns or textures. For vector field visualization, round spots are stretched in the direction of the 2D vector field before being deposited on the plane. He called this technique "spot noise". It is capable of showing fine detail in texture, while allowing another scalar variable to be represented by changing color. Unfortunately, it is only applied to 2D fields.

5.2.4 Volume Rendering

Crawfis and Max [CM92b] developed a technique to integrate volume rendering of a scalar field with a line segment representing a flow field. This was accomplished by sampling the dataset in back-to-front order on an image space voxel grid. At each point a scalar splat and vector line were drawn. The integration of the optical properties of the density cloud and the anti-aliased line segment was calculated for each pixel. The solution was entirely software based, but the visualizations of time-varying wind fields produced successful patterns for understanding these fields. Plate 18 (see color plate section) illustrates the wind field of a global climate simulation using this technique. The wind velocity is color-coded according to its position in the atmosphere. Don Dovey [Dov95] extend this technique to curvilinear and unstructured grids for representing a single flow field.

5.2.5 Line Integral Convolution

Cabral and Leedon [CL93] developed an algorithm that they called the Line Integral Convolution or LIC operator. It takes as input an n-dimensional vector field and an n-dimensional image. By using an image consisting of white noise (or band-limited noise), the algorithm will correlate the image in the direction of the vector field. It does this by taking the integral of the image along a local streamline subtended from each point in the output image (see Figure 5.3). The resolution of the input image, vector image and

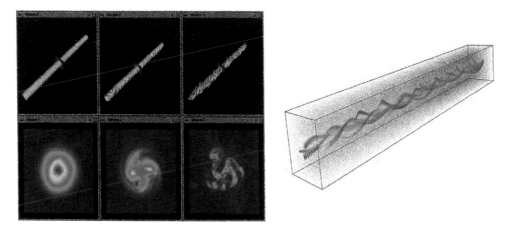

Plate 1 (Figure 1.1)

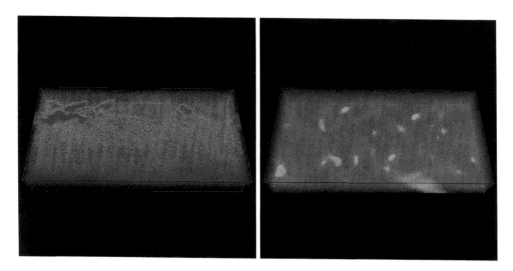

Plate 2 (Figure 1.2)

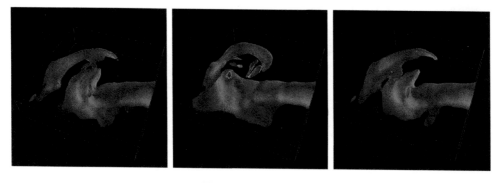

Plate 3 (Figure 1.4)

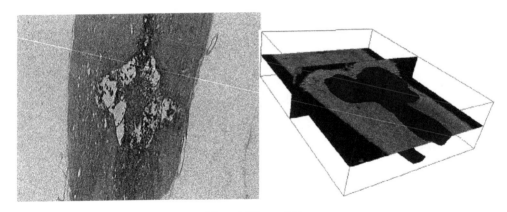

Plate 4 (Figure 1.5)

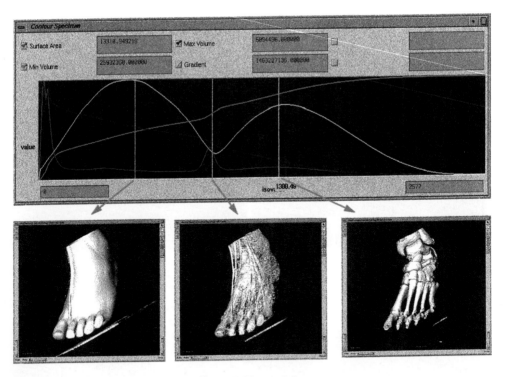

Plate 5 (Figure 1.6)

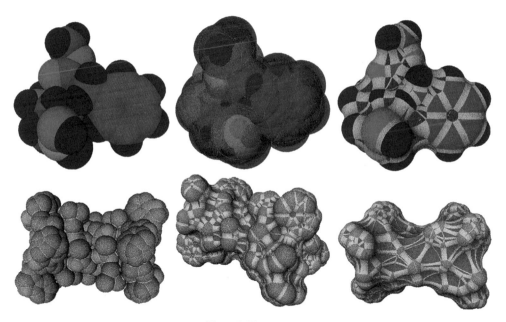

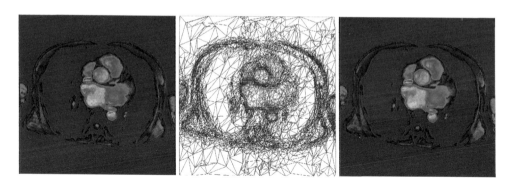

Plate 6 (Figure 1.7)

Plate 7 (Figure 1.8)

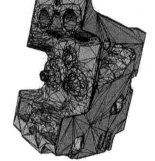

Plate 8 (Figure 1.9)

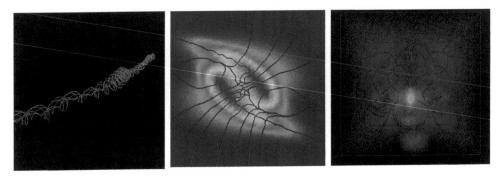

Plate 9 (Figure 10 (b))   Plate 10 (Figure 1.12)

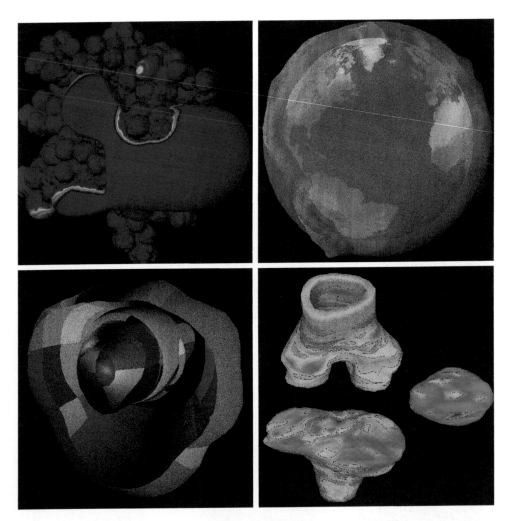

Plate 11 (Figure 1.13)

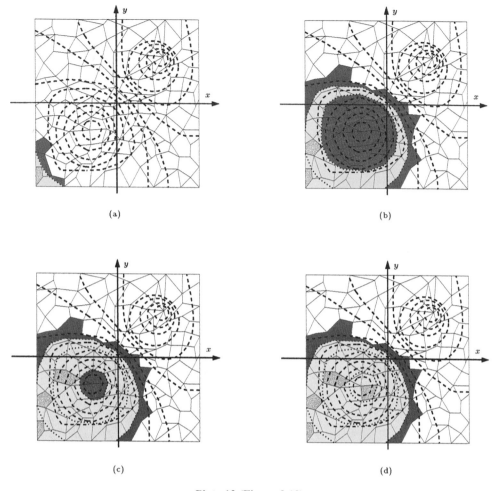

(a)

(b)

(c)

(d)

Plate 12 (Figure 3.13)

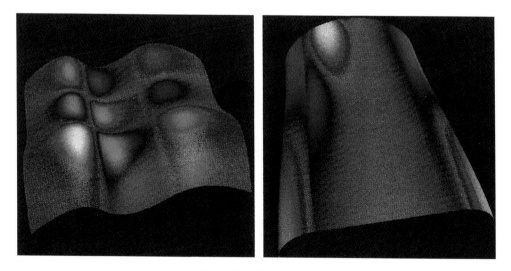

Plate 13 (Figure 4.22)

Plate 14

Plate 15

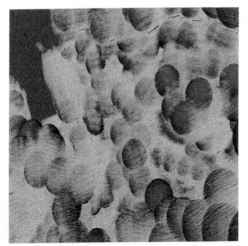

Plate 16

Plate 17

Plate 18

Plate 18 continued

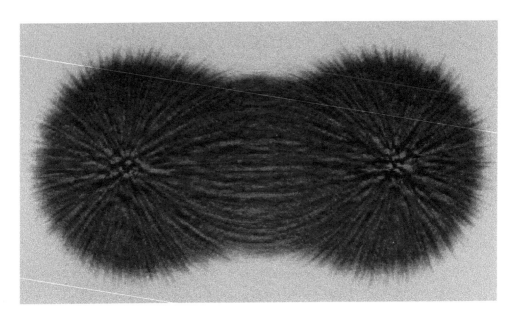

Plate 19

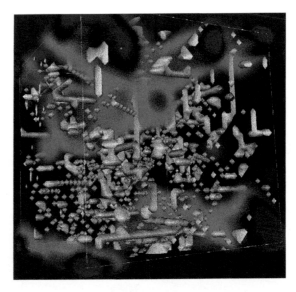

Plate 20 (Figure 6.1)

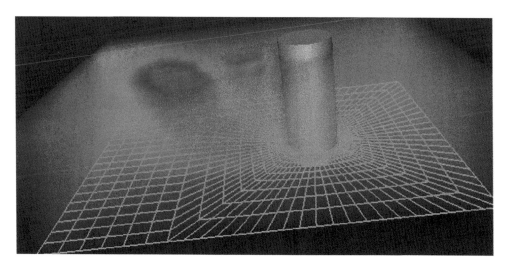

Plate 21 (Figure 6.2)

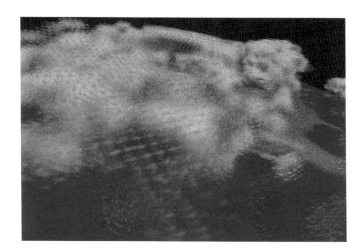

Plate 22 (Figure 6.3)

Plate 23 (Figure 6.4)

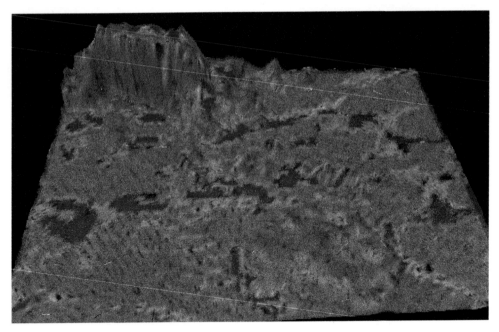

Plate 24 (Figure 6.7)

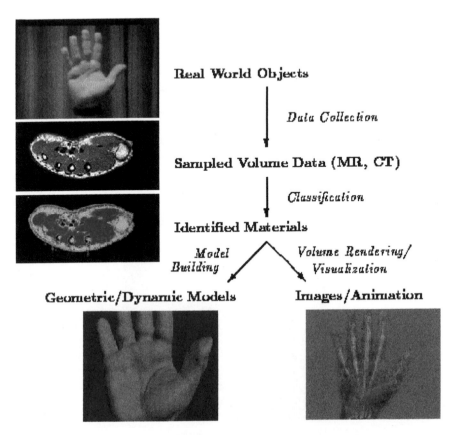

Plate 25 (Figure 7.2)

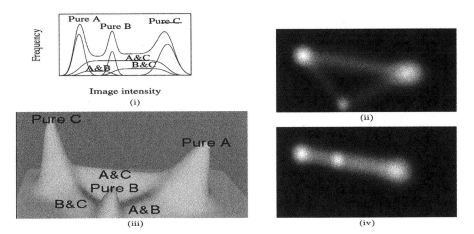

Plate 26 (Figure 7.6)

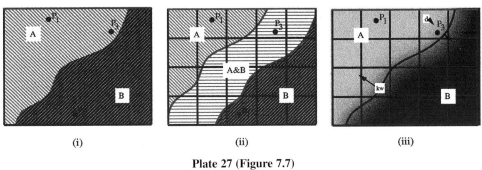

(i)   (ii)   (iii)

Plate 27 (Figure 7.7)

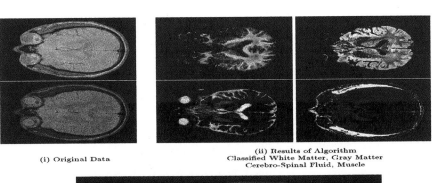

(i) Original Data

(ii) Results of Algorithm
Classified White Matter, Gray Matter
Cerebro-Spinal Fluid, Muscle

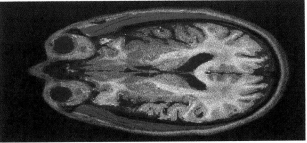

(iii) Combined Classified Image

Plate 28 (Figure 7.12)

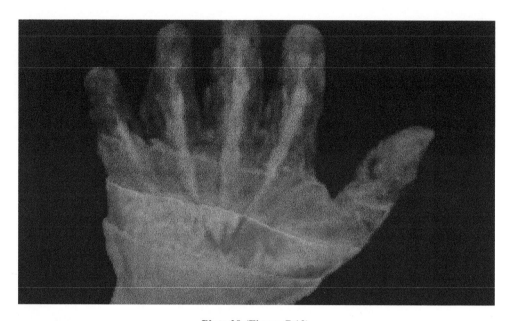

Plate 29 (Figure 7.13)

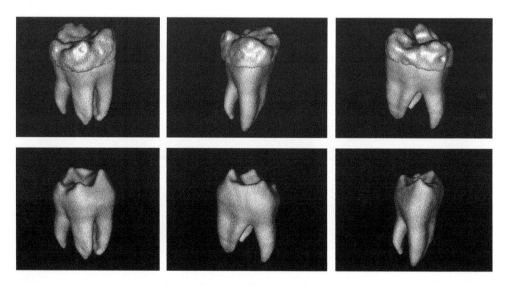

Plate 30 (Figure 7.14)

output image were all required to be the same in their implementation. The calculation of the stream lines requires the costly advection calculations described above. Since this is performed at every data point, the technique was quite slow. For 3D datasets, the resulting image still needed to be rendered. The authors chose to render using ray tracing which also added to the total cost of the algorithm. Plate 19 (see color plate section) uses a sample dipole field to illustrate this technique. Forssel [For94] extended the LIC operator to work on parametric slices (2D) of a curvilinear grid. The resulting 2D images were used as a texture map for the parametric slice. Stalling and Hege [SH95] improved the LIC algorithm as presented by Cabral and Leedom to be resolution independent and offer performance enhancements to speed up the running time.

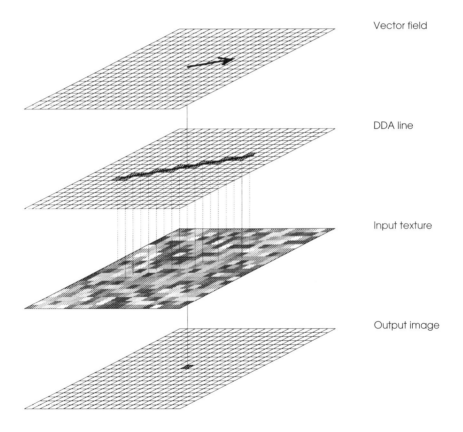

Figure 5.3 A small streamline is weighted with white noise and integrated to yield a single voxel intensity using the LIC technique. (Image courtesy of Brian Cabral and Lawrence Livermore National Laboratory.)

5.2.6   Textured Spats

The textured splat technique of Crawfis and Max [CM93] extends the volume rendering technique of splatting [Wes89, LH91] to represent flow fields by embedding tiny directional icons within the splat footprint. See Chapter 6, Section 6.4.1, this volume, for a more detailed description of the textured splat technique.

5.3   CLASSIFICATION TECHNIQUES

Classification or feature extraction techniques are also relatively new to scientific visualization. Hellman and Hesselink [HH91] have developed a technique to build stream surfaces to represent the topology of the flow. Globus, et al. [GLL91] have developed techniques to identify the critical points of a flow field. Iconic representations can be placed at these points with appropriate streamlines connecting them.

Banks and Singer [BS94], and Ma and Zheng [MZ94] present techniques that attempt to identify and represent vortex tubes resulting from turbulent flows.

Hanson and Ma [HM94] developed a technique based on the Frenet frame of a 3D space-curve that when mapped onto the surface of a sphere can show interesting correlations. The technique is more like a histogram, illustrating the distribution of directions, without illustrating where in the field individual directions occur.

6

Applications of Texture Mapping to Volume and Flow Visualization

Nelson Max
Lawrence Livermore National Laboratory

Roger Crawfis
The Ohio State University

Barry Becker
Silicon Graphics Inc.

ABSTRACT

We describe five visualization methods which take advantage of hardware polygon scan conversion, texture mapping, and compositing, to give interactive viewing of 3D scalar fields, and motion for 3D flows. For volume rendering, these are splatting of an optimized 3D reconstruction filter, and tetrahedral cell projection using a texture map to provide the exponential per pixel necessary for accurate opacity calculation. For flows, these are "splatting" of cycled anisotropic textures to provide flow direction and motion visualization, splatting motion blurred particles to indicate flow velocity, and advecting a texture directly to show the flow motion. All these techniques are tailored to take advantage of existing graphics pipelines to produce interactive visualization tools.

6.1 INTRODUCTION

Scientific visualization is necessary to understand the output of large-scale physical computer simulations in mechanics, hydrodynamics, and climate modeling. It is also useful in understanding data reconstructed from measurements such as MRI tomography and X-ray crystallography. One often wants to visualize a 2D or 3D scalar,

Data Visualization Techniques, Edited by C. Bajaj
© 1999 John Wiley & Sons Ltd

vector, or tensor field, or a steady or unsteady flow. Real-time animation is useful for understanding time-varying phenomena, and quick interaction and motion parallax are helpful in understanding 3D fields. These all demand fast rendering of the images.

In this chapter, we survey several rendering techniques we have recently developed, which achieve high speed by taking advantage of texture mapping hardware. Such hardware was originally developed for improved realism in training simulators, and is currently available on several high-end workstations. We expect it to become standard on future workstations, because of its ability to enhance image realism without increasing the complexity of geometric models.

In the following section, we briefly survey the concepts of texture mapping and compositing. Then in Section 6.3, we present two methods which use texture mapping to render 3D scalar volume densities. Section 6.4 describes two methods which use texture mapping to visualize vector fields or flows, based on combining small texture patterns. Section 6.5 discusses in greater detail a third such method, based on advecting larger texture patterns. Sections 6.1 through 6.4 are reprinted with permission from a paper with the same title as this chapter, in the *Proceedings of Graphicon '95*, Volume 1, pp. 108–113. Section 6.5 is reprinted with permission from "Flow Visualization using Moving Textures" in the *Proceedings of the ICASE/LaRC Symposium on Visualizing Time-Varying Data*, NASA Conference Publication 3321, pp. 77–87.

6.2   TEXTURE MAPPING

Texture mapping for computer graphics rendering was first done in software by Ed Catmull [Cat74]. It greatly enhances the apparent detail of an image, without increasing the number of graphics primitives like polygons or surface patches. The basic idea is to precompute or scan in a rectangular raster image representing the desired texture. The horizontal and vertical raster coordinates in this image are used as texture parameters. When a primitive is rendered, texture parameters for each image pixel are determined, and used to address the appropriate texture pixels. If the parameters vary smoothly across the surface, the texture appears to be applied to the surface. For example, on polygons, the texture parameters can be specified at the polygon vertices, and bilinearly interpolated in screen space (or in object space for better perspective projection during scan conversion). On triangles, bilinear interpolation is equivalent to linear interpolation. For smooth surface patches, the same u and v parameters used for the surface shape functions can also be used as texture parameters.

If the texture is a photograph complete with shading and shadows, it will not appear realistic when mapped to a curved surface. Therefore, the texture map is usually used to specify surface reflectivity, and then shading algorithms are applied.

Appropriate resampling is necessary when applying the texture to a surface. A surface pixel does not usually correspond exactly to a texture pixel, so its texture value should be a weighted average of several nearby pixels in the texture map. Heckbert [Hec86] and Wolberg [Wol90] describe a variety of anti-aliased resampling schemes. Here, we will describe the algorithms implemented in our workstation hardware. The texture parameters are interpolated with extra precision, so that the integer parts determine a texture pixel address, and the fractional parts determine fractional dis-

tances to the next adjacent pixel row or column. The fractional parts are then used
to compute weights for a bilinear combination of four adjacent texture pixels.

This scheme gives a smooth resampling in the case where the mapped texture pixels
are approximately the same size as the image pixels, and a smooth interpolation if
the mapped texture pixels are larger than the image pixels. However if the mapped
texture pixels are much smaller than the image pixels, some texture pixels which
should contribute to the image may be missed entirely, since each image pixel involves
at most four texture pixels. Lance Williams' MIP-mapping [Wil78] offers a partial
solution to this problem. From the original texture map, another map is made at half
the resolution, by averaging the pixel values in groups of four. The process is repeated,
to make maps of 1/4 resolution, 1/8 resolution, and so forth. Then when the texture is
used on a surface, an appropriate scale map is chosen, and the scheme of the previous
paragraph, using a weighted average of four adjacent pixels, is applied. In order to
prevent a sudden visible transition between two versions of the texture with different
scales, a weighted average of the two closest-scale maps may be used, giving in effect
a weighted average of eight texture map values.

One application for texture mapping is to render complicated shapes like trees,
clouds, or people, with a single polygon. This is done by storing both a color and an
opacity in the texture map. The opacity α is 1 minus the transparency, and varies
from 0 (completely transparent) to 1 (completely opaque). It is used to composite the
textured polygon over the background, using one of the following formulae:

$$\text{composite} \ = \ \alpha \cdot \text{color} \ + \ (1 - \alpha) \cdot \text{background} \qquad (6.1)$$

$$\text{composite} \ = \ \text{color} \ + \ (1 - \alpha) \cdot \text{background} \qquad (6.2)$$

See Porter and Duff [PD84] for a detailed explanation of these and other compositing
formulae. In order to get the appropriate transparency effects, the objects in the scene
must be sorted and composited in back-to-front order.

The five methods discussed below all involve compositing semi-transparent objects.
These objects can be combined with other opaque geometric objects in the scene,
without involving these opaque objects in the back-to-front sorting discussed below.
The opaque objects are rendered first, using a z-buffer to determine their visibility.
Then when compositing the semitransparent objects, their z is compared to the z-
buffer value to determine where the compositing should take place, but the z-buffer
value is not changed.

We used a Silicon Graphics Onyx, with two MIPS 4400 CPUs and a Reality Engine
graphics processor, in the work described below. This graphics processor performed
in hardware all the texturing and compositing algorithms described above, including fractional-precision texture coordinates for texture interpolation, MIP-mapping,
color/opacity texturing, compositing, flexible z-buffer testing/updating options multiplication of texture map values by separate transparency, and color shading values
interpolated from the polygon vertices. Similar capabilities are offered on hardware
from Kubota, Evans and Sutherland, and other manufactures, and are expected to
soon become available on less expensive platforms, in order to support video games.

6.3   VOLUME RENDERING

The goal of volume rendering is to produce an image of a varying density volume by projecting it on to an image plane. The color and opacity at a point in the volume can be specified as functions of a 3-D scalar field being visualized, and may also involve the gradient of the scalar field, the lighting direction, and the values of the scalar at other distant points. A survey of optical models for volume rendering is given in [Max95]. The basic ray tracing method for volume rendering integrates the color along a ray from the viewpoint passing through each pixel center, and continuing on into the volume. This integration must take account of the accumulating opacity along the ray, and compute

$$I = \int_0^D \text{color}(x(s)) \exp\left(-\int_0^s \text{opacity}(x(t))dt\right)ds \qquad (6.3)$$

where $x(s)$ is the point at a distance s from the viewpoint along the ray, D is the distance to the edge of the data volume or to the first completely opaque object, and

$$\exp\left(-\int_0^s \text{opacity}(x(t))dt\right)$$

is the transparency of the volume between the viewpoint and $x(s)$, which partially hides the color $(x(s))$ emitted at $x(s)$. See [Max95] for a derivation of equation (6.3) and the standard efficient algorithms for estimating the integral by sampling along the ray. If the color and opacity values are only determined at the vertices of a volume grid, these values must be interpolated at the sample points on the ray.

   An alternative to ray tracing is to project and composite semi-transparent volume elements in back-to-front order onto the image plane. The basic difference between projection methods and ray tracing methods is in the order of the loops over image pixels and volume data elements. For ray tracing, the outer loop is over the image pixels, and the inner loop is over the data elements along the ray. For projection, the outer loop is over the data elements, and the inner loop is over the image pixels they effect. This section discusses two techniques for using hardware texture mapping in projection methods. The ideal projection method should be mathematically equivalent to the ray tracing integral (6.3).

6.3.1   Splatting

In splatting, the first of our hardware assisted projection methods, the data elements are vertices of a regular grid. The splatting technique of Westover [Wes89] considers the continuous volume density as a weighted sum

$$W(x, y, z) = \sum_i \sum_j \sum_k h(x - i, y - j, z - k)V(i, j, k) \qquad (6.4)$$

where i, j, and k are indices for an integer grid vertex, $V(i, j, k)$ is the data value at that vertex, $W(x, y, z)$ is the interpolated value at a general non-integer point (x, y, z), and $h(u, v, w)$ is the weighting function, sometimes called the reconstruction kernel, describing the influence of each data value in the continuous interpolation. Practical

$h(u, v, w)$ have small compact support, so only a few terms in the sum (6.4) will have nonzero weights. For trilinear interpolation

$$h(u, v, w) = (1 - |u|)(1 - |v|)(1 - |w|) \tag{6.5}$$

and only eight nonzero terms are involved.

Westover proposed integrating $h(u, v, w)$ along the viewing direction, to get a function

$$f(u, v) = \int_{-\infty}^{\infty} h(u, v, w) dw \tag{6.6}$$

of only two variables, representing the influence of a single nonzero data value on the plane. This 2D projection of the weighting function is called a splat. The splat $f(u, v)$ is stored at high resolution in a texture map. During rendering, the grid vertices are processed from back to front. For each vertex, the values for f at the pixels it influences are retrieved (or interpolated) from the texture map, and multiplied by the color and opacity values for the vertex to get values to use in the compositing equations (6.1). Westover [Wes89] did this in software, but we did it using the texture mapping and compositing hardware in our workstation.

There are some problems with the method described above. One often wishes to rotate the data volume, so that the resulting motion parallax gives visual cues about the 3D distribution of the volume density. In fact, interactive rotation was the original motivation for the splatting technique. However, the standard trilinear weights in equation (6.5) are not rotationally symmetric, so a separate integration as in equation (6.6) would be needed for each new orientation, and the orientations even vary within a single frame in the case of perspective projection. Therefore a rotationally invariant weighting function is desired.

Westover proposed using a Gaussian function

$$h(u, v, w) = \exp(-(u^2 + v^2 + w^2)/\sigma^2)$$

which is rotationally symmetric, and has the simple integral

$$f(u, v) = \int_{-\infty}^{\infty} h(u, v, w) dw = \sigma\sqrt{\pi} \exp(-(u^2 + v^2)/\sigma^2) \tag{6.7}$$

This function does not have compact support, so it must be truncated to make a reasonably sized texture. Laur and Hanrahan [LH91] approximated the Gaussian (6.7) by a piecewise linear function, whose effect on the image could be produced by compositing a collection of triangles with linearly varying color and opacity. This could be done with standard scan conversion and compositing hardware, without the need for texture mapping. However, Mach bands are visible at the triangle edges. When rendering a volume as a composition of splats, they should blend together so that the individual splats are not visible. In an ideal situation, the sum (6.4) should be constant if all the data values $V(i, j, k)$ are constant, which requires that

$$\sum_i \sum_j \sum_k h(x - i, y - j, z - k) = 1 \tag{6.8}$$

This will be the case if the trilinear interpolation weighting (6.5) is used, but can never be the case for a rotationally symmetric splat. Nevertheless, there are splats of small finite support which are superior to Gaussians in this regard. In [CM93] we derived a piecewise cubic function

$$h(r) = h\left(\sqrt{u^2 + v^2 + w^2}\right)$$

which was constrained to be C^1 and optimized to make the sum (6.8) as constant as possible. It is

$$h(r) = \begin{cases} 0.557526 - 1.157743r^2 + 0.671033r^3 & 0 \le r \le s \\ 0.067599(t - r)^2 + 0.282474(t - r)^3 & s \le r \le t \\ 0. & t \le r \end{cases}$$

with $s = 0.889392$ and $t = 1.556228$. With this $h(r)$ the sum (6.8) deviates from 1.0 by only 0.25%. Figure 6.1 (Plate 20) shows a slowly varying scalar function volume rendered with the integral (6.6) of this splat in the texture map. For each data point in back-to-front order, a small square polygon was oriented perpendicular to the viewing ray, and composited into the image using hardware texture mapping, with z-buffer testing against a previously rendered opaque surface.

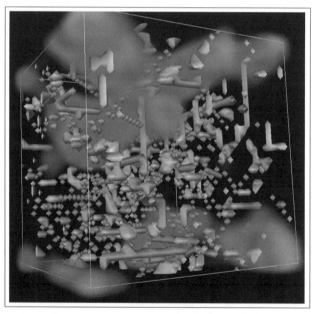

Figure 6.1 Air flow velocity through an aerogel, indicated by splats composited using z-buffer comparisons over opaque objects representing the aerogel. (See also color Plate 20)

The volume rendering appears smooth in this case. However if the vertex data represents point samples of a function with a discontinuity, individual splats may be visible near the discontinuity surface, giving a jagged staircase effect similar to the aliasing that occurs when point samples are taken at pixel centers near an intensity discontinuity in a 2D image. Once this is done, no reconstruction kernel can eliminate the aliasing. Instead, the image must be appropriately filtered before sampling to eliminate high frequencies, so that each sample data value is a weighted integral of intensities near the pixel center. The same sort of filtering should be used when taking 3D samples to be used in 3D reconstruction. Sometimes this filtering comes automatically when the data are observed. For example, data samples from X-ray crystallography come from inverse Fourier transforms of measured diffraction intensities, and can easily be band limited, and tomographic densities determined by CAT or MRI scans are averages determined by the limited spatial resolution of the detectors and of the mathematical reconstruction. In other cases, when the density function is defined mathematically or from a geometric model, filtering must be done by integration around each sample point.

Another problem with splatting is that it does not exactly correspond to the integral (6.3). The back-to-front compositing means that the contributions from equation (6.6) to the colored intensity for a single splat will not contain opacity effects from that splat or any others that have previously been composited. The transparency factor

$$\exp\left(-\int_0^s \operatorname{opacity}(x(t))dt\right)$$

accumulated by the compositing process only includes effects from splats that are subsequently composited over the current one. This may not be noticeable in a single image, but when a volume is rotated, the sorting order may change, causing the image to jump visibly, particularly if different colored splats are adjacent. Westover [Wes90] suggested a way to avoid much of this jumping. Among the three possible coordinate plane orientations in the (i, j, k) lattice, the one most perpendicular to the viewing direction is chosen. For each lattice plane in this orientation, in back-to-front order, splats are used to sum (rather than composite) both the color and opacity into a temporary color/opacity image, and these resampled images are composited as a whole. This eliminates all mutual opacity effects between splats in the same lattice plane. However, at some point during a rotation, the selection of the coordinate plane most perpendicular to the viewing direction will change, and a much stronger jump might result.

This modification could not be implemented easily on our hardware, since the hardware compositing only uses data coming down the graphics pipeline. Thus each color/opacity plane could be produced in hardware, but it would then need to be composited in software, or loaded into the texture map memory as a texture on one large polygon. Neither of these alternatives is fast, so we chose to composite each splat separately as in [Wes89]. A different scheme, using a three-dimensional texture map, evaluated on planes parallel to the view plane, is described in [CCF94].

6.3.2   Polyhedron Compositing

Instead of compositing splats for the data points, an alternative is to composite polyhedra joining the data points. Inside each polyhedron, the scalar field is interpolated from the data values given at its vertices. If the polyhedra can be correctly sorted in back-to-front order, equation (6.3) can be integrated separately along the viewing ray segments in each polyhedron. Garrity [Gar90] has shown how to trace a ray through a collection of polyhedral cells provided that one knows which cell, if any, is on the other side of every face in the current cell.

This topological information is also useful for doing a global back-to-front sort on the cells. In [MHC90] we considered the directed graph whose edges correspond to the cell faces, and are directed from the cell on the viewpoint side of the face plane to the other cell on the side facing away from the viewpoint. If the data volume is convex, with no holes or concavities, a topological sort of this graph (see [Knu73]) produces a back-to-front sort of the cells if one is possible, or determines that it is impossible, in time $O(n)$, where n is the number of cells and faces. Edelsbrunner [Ede89] has shown that for a Delaunay triangulation, this sort will always succeed. If data are available at irregularly spaced points, with no preferred meshing into cells, the Delaunay triangulation is thus a good choice, and is also preferred because the resulting tetrahedra have good shape properties.

For volumes with holes or concavities, Williams [Wil92] has supplemented this topological sort with a separate sort on the exterior cells which have free faces (with no adjacent cell) facing towards the viewpoint, but his method is not guaranteed to give the correct answer. A more sophisticated sort of the exterior cells, which is guaranteed to be corect, is given in [SMW98]. Stein, et al. [SBM94] gives a general sort which requires no topological information and is always correct when any sort exists, but it takes time $O(n^2)$. This sorting algorithm is also presented in [WMS98], with a correction and a speedup based on dividing the image plane into tiles. Max [Max93b] gives special sorts for some restricted geometries.

For polyhedral environments, polyhedron compositing [MHC90] is potentially more efficient than ray tracing [Gar90], because if the inner loop is over the cells, the scan conversion of the cells can take advantage of vertical and horizontal coherence. Max, et al. [MHC90] show how to do this for a convex cell by scan converting the front faces into one z-buffer, and the back faces into another. Lucas [Luc92] and Max [Max93a] show how a global z-buffer eliminates the need for the back face buffer, provided there are no holes in the volume.

After scan conversion into the front and back z-buffers, one must calculate for each affected pixel the integral (6.3) along the ray segment inside the cell. For a volume density $\rho(x)$ of particles whose color C and opacity τ are constant within the cell, $\text{color}(x) = C\rho(x)$, and $\text{opacity}(x) = \tau\rho(x)$, and the integral (6.3) reduces to

$$
\begin{aligned}
I &= \int_0^D C\rho(x(s)) \exp\left(-\int_0^s \tau\rho(x(t))dt\right) ds \\
&= -\frac{C}{\tau} \int_0^D (-\tau\rho(x(s))) \exp\left(-\int_0^s \tau\rho(x(t))dt\right) ds \\
&= -\frac{C}{\tau}\frac{d}{ds} \exp\left(-\int_0^s \tau\rho(x(t))dt\right) ds \qquad (6.9) \\
&= -\frac{C}{\tau} \exp\left(-\int_0^s \tau\rho(x(t))dt\right)\Bigg|_{s=0}^{s=D} \\
&= \frac{C}{\tau}\left(1 - \exp\left(-\int_0^D \tau\rho(x(t))dt\right)\right)
\end{aligned}
$$

The ratio C/τ can be interpreted as the surface glow color of the particles. (See [Max95].) If $\rho(x)$ is trilinearly interpolated from the cell vertices, as in a 3D version of Gouraud shading, with the viewing direction being one of the interpolation directions, then $\rho(x(s)))$ will vary linearly in s, so that the integral in (6.9) reduces to

$$I = \frac{C}{\tau}(1 - T) \qquad (6.10)$$

with the transparency

$$T = \exp\left(-\frac{D}{2}\tau(\rho(x(0)) + \rho(x(D)))\right) \qquad (6.11)$$

where $x(0)$ and $x(D)$ are the entry and exit points of the viewing ray for the cell. Equation (6.10) can be used in the standard compositing formula (6.1) with opacity $\alpha = 1 - T$, and object color C/τ.

The remaining two directions for the trilinear interpolation are along scanlines, and vertically between scanlines, and $\rho(x(0))$ and $\rho(x(D))$ can be bilinearly interpolated across the front and rear faces of the cell by standard scan conversion hardware. However, an exponential per pixel is still required for equation (6.11).

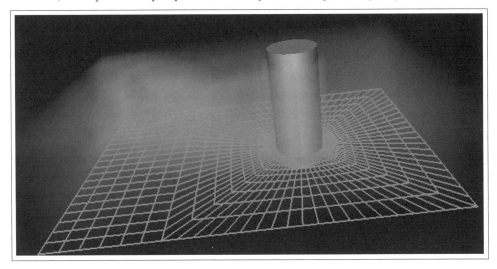

Figure 6.2 z-component of vorticity for water flow past a cylinder, rendered by compositing tetrahedra, using z-buffer comparison with the cylinder. (See also color Plate 21)

Here, finally, is where texture mapping can help. We subdivide the screen projection of a cell into polygons bounded by projected cell edges. Each such polygon is the projection of a prismatic region of the cell bounded on the front by a single front-facing cell face, and on the rear by a single back-facing cell face. The quantities $u = D$ and $v = \tau(\rho(x(0)) + \rho(x(D)))/2$ then vary linearly across each such polygon. They are specified at the polygon vertices, and linearly interpolated as texture parameters by the scan conversion and texture mapping hardware. Then, in the texture table, we put the opacity $\alpha = 1 - T = 1 - \exp(-uv)$, which is used by the texture compositing hardware. Thus equations (6.10) and (6.11) are compatible with the graphics hardware pipeline.

The only software component of this scheme is the subdivision into polygons of the cell's projection. Wilhelms and van Gelder [vGW93] give a line sweep algorithm for doing this for a general cell. In our initial implementation, we divided all cells into tetrahedra, and used the simpler scheme of Shirley and Tuchman [ST90] to subdivide the projected tetrahedra into triangles. In their hardware rendering, Shirley and Tuchman linearly interpolated α itself across the tetrahedra instead of doing the exponential per pixel. As demonstrated in [SBM94] and [MBC93], this approximation can lead to Mach bands, while our texture mapping scheme gives smooth images. Figure 6.2 (Plate 21) shows a finite element model, where the color indicates the z-component of the vorticity.

In applications like this where the color is specified separately at each vertex, equation (6.10) is not valid, because the color C is not constant across the viewing ray segment in a cell. Williams and Max [WM92] show how to calculate the integral in equation (6.9) when the color $C(x)$ and the particle density $\rho(x)$ both vary linearly along the ray. There are too many parameters in this calculation to be used as texture table indices, so the color must be calculated in software. To produce Figure 6.2 (Plate 21), we used the correct color only at the vertices of the screen projection triangles, and let the hardware interpolate it across the triangles. Only one vertex in the screen subdivision of each tetrahedron's projection corresponds to a ray segment for which color integration is required. The others, along the profile of the projection, correspond to single tetrahedron vertices where the color is already known.

We have now extended these methods from the tetrahedra to arbitrary convex polyhedra. See [WMS98] for details.

6.4   FLOW VISUALIZATION

We now describe three techniques for flow visualization which use texture mapping hardware. The goal is to produce animations which indicate the flow velocity.

6.4.1   Textured Splats

The splats of Section 6.3.1 were generalized by Crawfis and Max [CM93], to indicate velocity direction, by using an anisotropic texture. The texture has streaks resembling motion blurred particles which grow brighter in the direction of motion, towards the right in the texture map. As with the scalar splats, these vector splats are rendered with small texture mapped squares, perpendicular to the viewing direction. But now these squares are oriented so that the streaks point in the projected vector direction. By taking advantage of the flexible arithmetical combination of polygon vertex color and opacity with texture map color and opacity available in our workstation hardware, we were able to render both a scalar variable and a vector variable in a single splat. (See [CM93] for details.)

In addition, we were able to make the texture move in real time to animate the flow. We used a cycle of separate texture maps. In each successive frame, the motion blurred particles in the texture move farther to the right, fading out and exiting the texture square on the right, and reentering at the left. Each frame in the animation accessed the appropriate map in the texture cycle, so that the texture moved continuously in the flow. Even if there were too many splats to render in real time, we could rapidly accumulate the cycle of frames in the workstation memory, and then view them as an infinite loop. Figure 6.3 (Plate 22) shows an example of this technique.

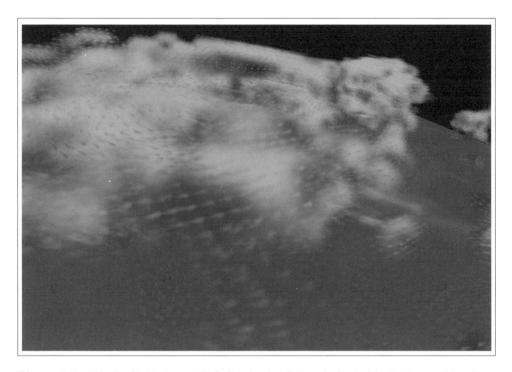

Figure 6.3   Wind velocity in a global climate simulation, indicated by texture splats whose scalar component indicates percent cloudiness. (See also color Plate 22)

6.4.2   Spot Noise

Van Wijk [vW91], [vW93a] has used small motion blurred particles to visualize flows on stream surfaces. The particles were represented as ellipses with their long axes oriented along the direction of flow. They were composited in software. In [MCG94], we used hardware texture mapping to render and composite these ellipses.

A basic texture was defined on a square, to give a blurred circular spot. Then, instead of texturing a square oriented normal to the viewing ray, we used a rectangle, whose long side was oriented along the flow velocity vector. This turned the projected spot into a stretched ellipse, whose long axis increased with increasing projected velocity. The particles were advected by the flow, so that they indicated the flow velocity in animation. By advecting and rendering only the particles near a contour surface, we were able to produce real-time animation. Figure 6.4 (Plate 23) shows particles near a surface of constant velocity magnitude, from a simulation of air flow through a filter.

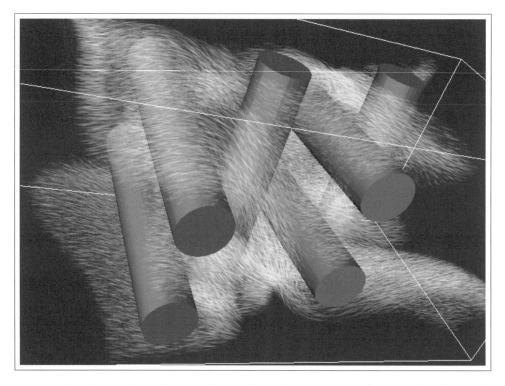

Figure 6.4 Spot noise indicating air flow through an air filter. (See also color Plate 23)

6.5   TEXTURE ADVECTION

An intuitive way to visualize a flow is to watch textures move in the flow. The early color table animation of [Sho79] was an example of this technique. The LIC method [CL93, For94] uses integrals of white noise textures along streamlines, moving the weighting function in the integrals from frame to frame to animate the texture motion, see Chapter 5, Section 5.2.5. Initially, LIC was applied mainly to 2D flows, but Forssell [SH95] has used texture mapping hardware to apply a 2D LIC surface flow texture to the skin of a 3D airplane model. The directional texture blurring from the LIC integration creates anisotropic textures which indicate the flow even in a still frame. However they are computationally intensive, and cannot generate animation in real time. Here, we show how texture mapping hardware can produce near-real-time motion by advecting one fixed texture on a polygon grid. However, we make no attempt to indicate the flow direction in a still frame. As discussed below, any anisotropic stretching comes from the velocity gradient, not the velocity itself.

The basic idea is to advect the texture by the flow field. In [MCW92], we gave an indication of the wind velocity by advecting the 3D texture coordinates on the polygon vertices of a cloudiness contour surface in a climate simulation. This was slow, because the 3D texture was rendered in software, and because advecting the texture was difficult for time-varying flows. Here, we replace the 3D textures by 2D texture maps compatible with hardware rendering, and give techniques for handling time-varying flows more efficiently.

The next subsection gives our technique for 2D steady flows, and the one after that discusses the problems of texture distortion. Then we discuss the problems with extending our method to time-varying flows, and our two solutions. Finally, we develop compositing methods for visualizing 3D flows.

6.5.1   Steady 2D Flows

We start with a mathematical definition of texture advection, and then show how it can be approximated by hardware texture mapped polygon rendering. Let $V(x, y)$ be a steady (i.e., time-independent) velocity field to be visualized, and let $F^t(x, y)$ be the corresponding flow. This means that $F^t(x, y)$ is solution of the differential equation

$$\frac{dF^t}{dt} = V(F^t(x, y))$$

with initial condition $F^0(x, y) = (x, y)$. A point P is carried by the flow to the point $F^t(P)$ after a time delay t. The flow F^t satisfies the composition rule

$$F^{s+t}(P) = F^s(F^t(P)) \tag{6.12}$$

for both positive and negative s and t. Thus $(F^t)^{-1}(P) = F^{-t}(P)$.

Here, we will assume that the initial texture coordinates at $t = 0$ are the same as the (x, y) coordinates of the region R being rendered. In practice, the texture is usually defined in a different (u, v) coordinate system related to (x, y) by translation and scaling, but for simplicity we will ignore the difference.

If $T(x, y)$ is an initial 2D texture being advected by the flow, then at time t it is carried to a new texture $T_t(x, y)$ defined by

$$T_t(x, y) = T((F^t)^{-1}(x, y)) = T(F^{-t}(x, y))$$

Thus, to compute T_t at a point P, we go backwards along the streamline through P, to find the point Q such that $F^t(Q) = P$, and then evaluate the texture function T at Q. When animated, this will give the appearance that the initial texture T is being carried along by the flow. By equation (6.12) above, $F^{-(t+\Delta t)}(P) = F^{\Delta t}(F^{-t}(P))$. Thus the streamlines $F^{-t}(P)$ needed for the texture coordinates can be computed incrementally.

There are two problems with this formulation when the domain of definition for $V(x, y)$ or $T(x, y)$ is limited to a finite region R in which the velocity data or texture is available. First of all, if the streamline $F^{-t}(P)$ leaves the region R, the necessary velocities are not available to continue the integration. One must either extrapolate the known velocities outside R, or continue the streamline as a straight line using the last valid velocity. Fortunately, either of these extrapolation methods will give a correctly moving texture in animation. This is because the visible texture motion at a point P inside R is determined only by the velocity at P, and the extrapolation of the streamline beyond R serves only to determine what texture will be brought in from "off-screen".

Second, even if $F^{-t}(P)$ is extended outside R, the texture may not be known there. The standard solution to this is to take $T(x, y)$ to be a periodic function in both x and y, so that it is defined for all (x, y). Most texture mapping hardware is capable of generating this sort of wraparound texture, by using modular arithmetic (or truncation of high-order bits) to compute the appropriate texture map address from the x and y values. There are also tools to generate textures which wrap around without apparent seams [HB95].

To adapt this technique to hardware polygon rendering, the 2D region R is divided up into a regular grid of triangles, and the texture coordinates $F^{-t}(P_i)$ are only computed for the vertices P_i of the grid. During the hardware scan conversion, texturing, and shading process, the texture coordinates at each pixel are interpolated from those at the vertices, and the appropriate texture pixels are accessed.

6.5.2   Texture Distortion

The flow $F^{-t}(P)$ can change the shape of a triangle, so that it becomes long and thin in texture space, as shown in Figure 6.5. In the direction where the triangle is stretched by F^{-t}, the texture will be compressed by F^t. This distortion will not be present if the velocity is constant, so that F^{-t} and F^t are both translations. The distortion instead indicates anisotropies in the derivatives of V. For incompressible 2D flows, stretching in one direction will be compensated for by compression in a perpendicular direction. For compressible flows, there may be stretching in all directions at some positions, and shrinking in all directions at others.

During the animation of the texture advection, this distortion continues to build up, so that eventually the visualization becomes useless. Therefore we periodically restart the texture coordinates back at their original positions in the regular grid. To avoid the sudden jump this would cause in the animation, we gradually fade up the new texture and fade down the old one, according to the weighting curves in Figure 6.6.

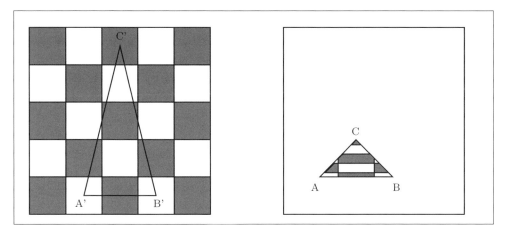

Figure 6.5   The triangle ABC on the right is mapped to the triangle A'B'C' in the texture on the left, so the texture ends up compressed vertically when triangle ABC is rendered.

Each texture starts with weight zero, fades up over the old texture until it alone is present, and then fades down as an even newer texture takes its place. This "cross dissolve" can be done in hardware, using the α compositing of equation (6.1). If the textures are random, and contain an adequate range of spatial frequencies, this cross dissolve will not disturb the perception of continuously flowing motion.

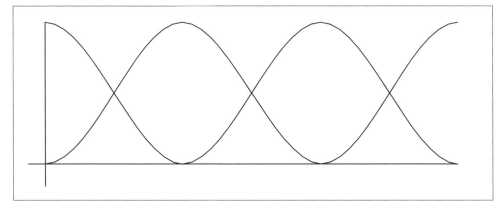

Figure 6.6   Three cycles of the weighting curves for fading the textures up and down.

Since each texture is used for only a short time, the distortion does not become extreme. For a steady flow, one cross dissolve cycle ends with the same image at which it began, so an animation loop may be created which can be cycled rapidly and repeatedly on a workstation screen. Similar precomputed loops are possible with the surface particle [vW93a], LIC [CL93], and textured splat [CM93] techniques.

6.5.3   Unsteady 2D Flows

If the velocity V depends on t, the differential equation

$$\frac{dF^t}{dt} = V(F^t(x,y),t) \tag{6.13}$$

defines a flow which no longer satisfies equation (6.12). For a fixed initial position Q, the curve $F^t(Q)$ is a particle trace $C(t)$ as in [Lan94], rather than a streamline. To find the texture coordinates for P at time t_0 we need to find the point Q such that $F^t(Q) = P$. We must go backwards along the particle trace, and thus solve the differential equation

$$\frac{dC(t)}{dt} = V(C(t),t)$$

for the t range $0 \le t \le t_0$, with "final" condition $C(t_0) = P$, and then set $Q = C(0)$. With the change of variables $u = t_0 - t$, this is equivalent to the differential equation

$$\frac{dC(u)}{du} = -V(C(u), t_0 - u) \tag{6.14}$$

for the u range $0 \le u \le t_0$, with initial condition $C(0) = P$. Then $Q = C(t_0)$.

In the case of unsteady flow, the differential equations (6.14) for different t_0 are not related and define completely different particle traces, so incremental methods can no longer be used. In [MCW92] we integrated equation (6.14) anew for each frame time t_0. To find the texture coordinates for frame t_0, we had to access the time-varying velocity data for the whole t range $0 \le t \le t_0$, which is very inefficient for large data-sets. Here we propose two more practical methods.

The first method is to derive a differential equation for the flow $G^t(x,y) = (F^t)^{-1}$. This flow maps a point P to the texture coordinate point Q needed at frame time t, that is, the point with $F^t(Q) = P$. Thus we have

$$F^t(G^t(P)) = P. \tag{6.15}$$

Let G_x^t and G_y^t be the x and y components of the vector valued function $G^t(x,y)$, and similarly let F_x^t and F_y^t be the components of Ft. Then by differentiating the components of equation (6.15) with respect to t by the chain rule, and using the fact that P does not vary with t, we get the pair of equations

$$\frac{\partial F_x^t}{\partial x}\frac{\partial G_x^t}{\partial t} + \frac{\partial F_x^t}{\partial y}\frac{\partial G_y^t}{\partial t} + \frac{\partial F_x^t}{\partial t} = 0$$

$$\frac{\partial F_y^t}{\partial x}\frac{\partial G_x^t}{\partial t} + \frac{\partial F_y^t}{\partial y}\frac{\partial G_y^t}{\partial t} + \frac{\partial F_y^t}{\partial t} = 0$$

Now by equation (6.13), $\frac{\partial F_x^t}{\partial t} = V_x$ and $\frac{\partial F_y^t}{\partial t} = V_y$, where V_x and V_y are the components of the velocity field at position $G^t(P)$ and time t. Therefore we have

$$M\begin{pmatrix} \frac{\partial G_x^t}{\partial t} \\ \frac{\partial G_y^t}{\partial t} \end{pmatrix} = \begin{pmatrix} -V_x \\ -V_y \end{pmatrix}$$

where M is the Jacobian matrix for the flow $F^t(x, y)$:

$$M = \begin{bmatrix} \frac{\partial F^t_x}{\partial x} & \frac{\partial F^t_x}{\partial y} \\ \frac{\partial F^t_y}{\partial x} & \frac{\partial F^t_y}{\partial y} \end{bmatrix}$$

Thus

$$\begin{pmatrix} \frac{\partial G^t_x}{\partial t} \\ \frac{\partial G^t_y}{\partial t} \end{pmatrix} = M^{-1} \begin{pmatrix} -V_x \\ -V_y \end{pmatrix}$$

But since $G^t(x, y) = (F^t)^{-1}(x, y)$, the matrix M^{-1} is the Jacobian matrix J for $G^t(x, y)$:

$$J = \begin{bmatrix} \frac{\partial G^t_x}{\partial x} & \frac{\partial G^t_x}{\partial y} \\ \frac{\partial G^t_y}{\partial x} & \frac{\partial G^t_y}{\partial y} \end{bmatrix}$$

Thus $G^t(x, y)$ satisfies the partial differential equations:

$$\frac{\partial G^t_x(x, y)}{\partial t} = -\frac{\partial G^t_x(x, y)}{\partial x} V_x - \frac{\partial G^t_x(x, y)}{\partial y} V_y$$

$$\frac{\partial G^t_y(x, y)}{\partial t} = -\frac{\partial G^t_y(x, y)}{\partial x} V_x - \frac{\partial G^t_y(x, y)}{\partial y} V_y$$

(6.16)

These differential equations essentially say that the flow $G^t(x, y)$ is determined from the negative of the velocity V, as transformed into the texture coordinate system appropriate for $t = 0$, so they determine the texture flow necessary to give the desired apparent velocity at time t. For example, if the texture on the triangle ABC of Figure 6.5 is to flow in the direction AC, the texture coordinates must be incremented by a vector in the direction C'A'. The initial condition for G^t at $t = 0$ is that $G^0(P) = P$, that is, G^0 is the identity map. Equations (6.16) can be integrated incrementally in time by Euler's method. If $G^t(P_{ij})$ is known at time t for all vertices on a regular grid, the partials in the Jacobian matrix $J(P_{ij})$ can be estimated from central differences between the G^t values at adjacent grid vertices. (For vertices at the boundary of R, one-sided differences must be used.) Then, using the current velocity $V(G^t(P_i), t)$, increments $\Delta G_x = \frac{\partial G^t_x}{\partial t} \Delta t$ and $\Delta G_y = \frac{\partial G^t_y}{\partial t} \Delta t$ are found for the components of G^t from equation (6.16). If necessary, Δt can be a fraction of the time-step between frames, and/or the vertex grid used for solving equations (6.16) can be finer than the triangle grid used in rendering the texture, in order to make the solution more accurate.

The vertex grid spacing will affect the accuracy of the finite difference approximations to the partial derivatives like $\frac{\partial G^t_y}{\partial x}$. This accuracy is critical, because small errors in these partials will cause errors in position in the next frame, which may compound the errors in the partials, and cause them to grow exponentially from frame to frame. Here again, it is useful to fade out the current advected texture and fade in a new texture whose coordinates are reinitialized to the identity map, so that the integration errors cannot accumulate for too long.

The second method for handling unsteady flows is to move the triangle vertices by the flow $F^t(x, y)$, keeping their texture coordinates constant. This advects the texture directly, by moving the triangles, and carrying the texture along with them. To do this, we incrementally integrate equation (6.13), and no partial derivative estimates are needed for a Jacobian. However we again have a problem at the edges of the region R. The boundary vertices may move inside R, leaving gaps at the edges, or may move outside, causing too much texture to be rendered. The excess rendering is easily prevented by clipping all triangles to the boundary of R. The gaps can be eliminated by creating extra guard polygons around the edges of R, widening it to a larger region S. Whenever any vertex on the boundary of S crosses into R, a new row of guard polygons is added to the affected side of S. Again it is useful to integrate only over a limited time interval before reinitializing the texture coordinates, to avoid creating too many extra polygons.

6.5.4   Flows in 3D

In three dimensions, one could advect 3D texture coordinates, but 3D texturing is not widely available. We instead used 2D textures on parallel section planes. We made the textured planes semi-transparent, and composited them from back to front using the α compositing hardware in our workstation. For the methods which change only the texture coordinates, we used the 2D projection of the velocity onto the section plane. For the method which moves the triangle vertices, we used the true 3D velocity, allowing the section surfaces to warp out of planarity.

Combining the compositing for the cross-dissolve of Figure 6.6 with the compositing of the separate texture planes can lead to problems in the accumulated opacity. Given two objects with opacities α_1 and α_2, the resulting opacity from compositing both objects is $\alpha_1 + \alpha_2 - \alpha_1\alpha_2$. (See [PD84] or multiply the transparencies.) Suppose $f_1(t)$ and $f_2(t)$ are the two weighting curves shown in Figure 6.6, with $f_1 + f_2 = 1$, and α is the desired section plane opacity. If we just take the two component opacities to be $\alpha_1 = \alpha f_1$ and $\alpha_2 = \alpha f_2$, the result is a composite opacity

$$\alpha_C = \alpha f_1 + \alpha f_2 - \alpha^2 f_1 f_2 = \alpha - \alpha^2 f_1 f_2$$

The unwanted last term causes a periodic pulsation in α_C.

A solution is to use exponentials, which have better multiplicative properties. Define an "optical depth" $l = -\ln(1 - \alpha)$, so that $\alpha = 1 - e^{-l}$, and let $\alpha_1 = 1 - e^{-f_1 l}$ and $\alpha_2 = 1 - e^{-f_2 l}$. The resulting composite opacity is then

$$
\begin{aligned}
\alpha_C &= \alpha_1 + \alpha_2 - \alpha_1\alpha_2 \\
&= 1 - e^{-f_1 l} + 1 - e^{-f_2 l} - (1 - e^{-f_1 l})(1 - e^{-f_2 l}) \\
&= 1 - e^{-(f_1 + f_2)l} = 1 - e^{-l} = \alpha
\end{aligned}
$$

as desired.

Another problem with compositing texture planes of constant transparency is that the frontmost planes will eventually obscure the ones to the rear if the data volume gets large. One solution is to use variable-transparency textures, so that some regions of the texture are completely transparent. Another is to specify the transparency on triangle vertices using a separate scalar data variable which can select out regions of interest where the texture motion should be visible. In [MCW92], we used percent cloudiness contour surfaces to specify the location of the advecting software-rendered texture. With our new hardware based technique, this cloudiness variable is used to specify the vertex transparency, which the hardware multiplies by the texture transparency. It thus produces similar realism in much less time. Figure 6.7 (Plate 24) shows these techniques used to visualize clouds and winds over Australia and Southeast Asia. The texture is applied to several semi-transparent layered sheets of polygons, which curve over the exaggerated altitude variation of the terrain. Color and opacity both indicate percent cloudiness, with higher percent cloud cover in a layer corresponding to greater opacity. This is a frame from an animation showing the results of a climate simulation, and both the clouds and the wind velocity vary with time. The texture is advected by the winds, using the methods described above, including the integration of equation (6.16).

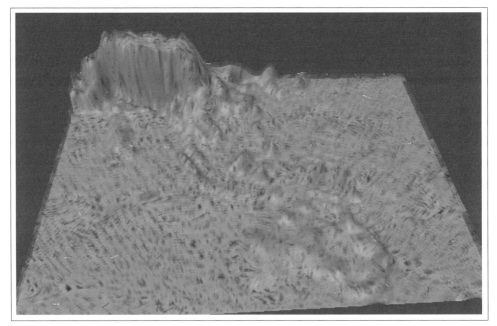

Figure 6.7   Clouds and wind flow over Southeast Asia and Australia. (See also color Plate 24)

ACKNOWLEDGMENTS

This work was performed under the auspices of the U.S. Department of Energy by Lawrence Livermore National Laboratory under contract number W-7405-ENG-48, with specific support from an internal LDRD grant. The sorting for Figure 6.2 (Plate 21) used an algorithm of Cliff Stein [SBM94]. The text of this chapter was initially typed by Fran Faria.

7

Continuous Bayesian Tissue Classification for Visualization

David H. Laidlaw

California Institute of Technology

ABSTRACT

This chapter discusses tissue classification – the identification of regions of materials in volume data. Our primary motivation is creating images for understanding biological systems from medical imaging data. We advocate an approach to this problem that avoids some of the pitfalls of approaches derived directly from discrete pattern recognition. By combining sampling theory and Bayesian probability theory, images can be generated without many of the aliasing artifacts otherwise introduced.

We first discuss the classification problem, its place in the visualization cycle, and some approaches to it. We then outline the approach we advocate. It involves reconstructing a continuous function from samples and examining the function over small, voxel-sized regions rather than at single points. The behavior of the continuous function over those regions provides much richer information and is the key to improving classification results. We discuss three algorithms and a framework for developing additional ones. Results of applying the algorithms to simulated and real MRI data show their efficacy.

7.1 INTRODUCTION

Visualization is inherently an iterative process that must be coupled with scientific questions to be meaningful. Figure 7.1 shows the cycle, starting with a hypothetical model for some physical phenomenon, continuing with observation and collection of data, and finishing (one iteration) with visualization and analysis of the data. The ultimate goal of the process is to converge on insight and understanding of the phenomenon under study.

Data Visualization Techniques, Edited by C. Bajaj
© 1999 John Wiley & Sons Ltd

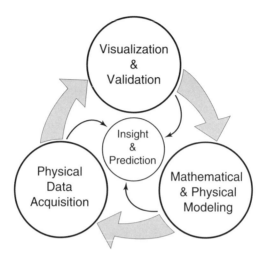

Figure 7.1 Scientific visualization cycle.

Geometry is at the heart of visualization, and extracting geometry from scientific measurements is a central part of scientific visualization. The goal of our visualization process is the understanding of the development and anatomy of biological systems through the study of their geometry. We describe here one stage in a three-stage computational framework for extracting geometry from sampled volume data. Within the framework, shown in Figure 7.2 (Plate 25), we measure the biological systems, identify different regions within them, and create images and models using information about the regions and the measurement process.

Tissue classification or segmentation, the second step of the framework, is the focus of this chapter. We will describe how the search for geometry impacts the classification process, the algorithmic changes it leads to, a framework for creating new algorithms that work well for extracting geometry, and some examples of new algorithms.

These techniques convert unclassified volume images into volume images with a physical interpretation that is more appropriate for many visualization algorithms. Resulting images may measure, for example, the local density of a material or the distance from a boundary between materials. The physical interpretation of these volume images is appropriate for volume rendering [Lev88b] (see Chapter 2), extraction of surface models [LC87] (see Chapter 3), and extraction of volume models. With these images and models we hope to be able to address anatomical and developmental questions through examination of systems and through predictive modeling of complex biological shapes and behavior. Applications also exist for surgical planning and assistance, conventional computer animation, and other imaging modalities.

7.1.1 Related Work

Many researchers have worked on identifying the locations of materials in sampled datasets [VBJ+85, VSR88, CLKJ90, DH73]. [CVC+95] gives an extensive review of the segmentation of MRI data. However, many of these algorithms generate artifacts

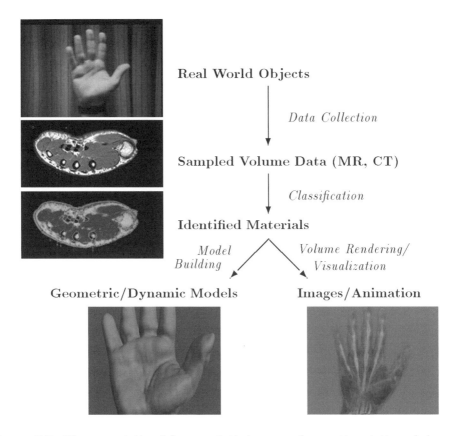

Figure 7.2 The computational framework that we use for creating static and dynamic geometric models of biological systems from MRI data. Our focus is on the second stage, tissue classification. (See also color Plate 25)

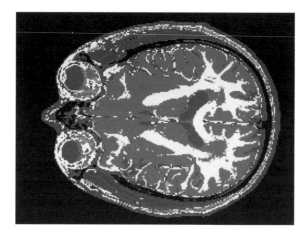

Figure 7.3   Discrete, single-material classification of the same human brain slice shown in Figure 7.12. (See also color Plate 28)

like those shown in Figure 7.3, an example of data classified with a technique based on discrete sample values. These techniques work well in regions where a voxel contains only a single material, but tend to break down at boundaries between materials. This introduces both stair-step artifacts, as shown between gray matter and white matter within the brain, and thin layers of misclassified voxels, as shown by the white matter between the skull and the skin. Both types of artifacts can be ascribed to the partial-volume effects ignored by the segmentation algorithms.

A number of algorithms address this limitation of discrete classification techniques. [DCH88] demonstrates that accounting for mixtures of materials within a voxel can reduce these artifacts, and approximates the relative volume of each material represented by a sample as the probability that the sample is that material. The technique works well for differentiating air, soft tissue, and bone in CT data, but not for differentiating materials in MR data, where the measured data value for one material may often be identical to the measured value for a mixture of two other materials. [WAAR+88] and [KSW96] avoid partial-volume artifacts by taking linear combinations of components of vector measurements. An advantage of their techniques is that the linear operations they perform preserve the partial-volume mixtures within each sample value, and so partial-volume artifacts are not created. A disadvantage is that the linear operations are not as powerful as nonlinear operations, and so either more data must be acquired or classification results may not be as accurate. [CHK91] and [NFMD90] address the partial-volume issue by identifying combinations of materials for each sample value. As with many other approaches to identifying mixtures, these techniques use only a single measurement taken within a voxel to represent its contents. Without the additional information available within each voxel region, these classification algorithms are limited in their accuracy. [SG93] share a mixture distribution for histograms with our technique. Their technique, however, estimates material amounts in an entire dataset, and does not classify the data at a voxel level.

[WCW88] present an interesting approach to partial-volume imaging that makes assumptions similar to ours about the underlying geometry being measured and about the measurement process. The results of their algorithm are a discrete material as-

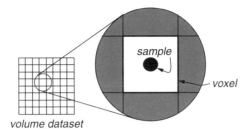

Figure 7.4 We define a sample as a scalar- or vector-valued element of a multi-dimensional dataset. A voxel is the region surrounding a sample.

signment for each sub-voxel of the dataset. Taken collectively, these multiple sub-voxel results provide a measure of the mixtures of materials within a voxel but arrive at it in a very different manner than does our algorithm. This work has been applied to satellite imaging data, and so results are difficult to compare, but aspects may combine well with our technique.

7.1.2 Continuous Classification

We have developed a methodology for constructing a probabilistic Bayesian classification algorithm from a set of assumptions about the underlying data. Our algorithms start with the premise that the sampled datasets satisfy the sampling theorem, which allows us to reconstruct a continuous function $\rho(x)$ over the entire dataset [OWY83]. We treat a voxel as a volume of space (see Figure 7.4). We examine all the values that the reconstructed function takes on over a voxel by calculating histograms of $\rho(x)$ over small regions of the dataset and classify those histograms by fitting histogram basis functions constructed from the set of assumptions. This approach builds upon statistical classification and nonlinear digital image and signal processing.

Using the Bayesian framework, we have constructed three different classification algorithms, described in more detail below. The first algorithm models the contents of each voxel as a linear combination of pure materials and mixtures of two materials. The second algorithm models each voxel as either entirely composed of a single pure material, or composed of two materials with a separating boundary. The third algorithm is substantially similar to the second, but allows the expected value, or signature, of each material to vary over a dataset, a common characteristic of MRI data. These techniques classify MRI data better than previously available techniques because they use a more accurate model of the collected data. They are also tailored to produce accurate results near boundaries between materials where extracted geometric details are most visible.

7.1.3 Organization of Chapter

In Section 7.2 we describe a Bayesian framework for developing new classification algorithms. As we present each step in the framework, we work through a simple example to illustrate the process. Section 7.3 gives an overview of the family of algorithms that we have developed using the framework. They are described in more detail in [Lai95], [LBJ97], [GLF+95], and [LFB97].

We show some results of visualizing volume data classified with our techniques in Section 7.4. Our visualizations take two basic forms, surface rendering and volume rendering. Most traditional computer graphics imagery is rendered as surfaces, although in the last decade volume rendering has emerged as a useful adjunct to the more traditional techniques. Unlike surface rendering methods, volume rendering produces images that can show internal structure. Thus, images of solid objects can appear to consist of volumes of transparent or semi-transparent material (see Chapter 2).

7.2   A FRAMEWORK FOR CLASSIFICATION SOLUTIONS

We define a statistical framework for creating classification algorithms. It is based on Bayesian probability theory [Lor90] and approximations of conditional and prior probabilities. Within the framework we have created a family of new algorithms that calculate the probability of a particular combination of materials given the histogram over a small region. We then find the most likely combination for the region.

In this section we outline how to construct a new classification algorithm within our framework, illustrating the process with an existing algorithm. We begin by defining terms.

7.2.1   Definitions

We refer to the coordinate system of the space of the object we are measuring as *spatial coordinates* and generally use $x \in X$ to refer to points. X is n_x-dimensional, where n_x is 3 for volume data, but can be 2 for slices.

Each measurement, or *sample* (see Figure 7.4), may be a scalar or vector and lies in *feature space* (see Figure 7.5), with points frequently denoted as $v \in V$. Feature space is n_v-dimensional, where n_v is 1 for scalar-valued data, 2 for two-element vector data, etc.

From the samples we reconstruct a continuous function $\rho(x)$ over X by interpolating sample values. We use tricubic interpolation and so incorporate information from 64 nearby samples into each interpolated measurement. A *voxel*, or *voxel region* (see Figure 7.4), is the volume surrounding a sample. The terms are interchangeable. We use voxels that tile the volume of a dataset, but overlapping or nonadjacent voxels are also possible. We are frequently interested in the behavior of $\rho(x)$ over the region defined by the volume of a voxel.

Classification algorithms classify a voxel based on information derived from the raw data in or near the voxel. We refer to the information as *voxel-info*, and label it h. For each of our classification techniques we use a histogram over the small region defined by a voxel to encode the information contained in the voxel. We first reconstruct a continuous function over the entire dataset from the samples and then use the continuous analog of a discrete histogram,

$$h^{\mathcal{R}}(v) = \int \mathcal{R}(x)\delta(\rho(x) - v)dx \qquad (7.1)$$

to calculate a histogram over each voxel. $\mathcal{R}(x)$ is nonzero within the region of interest, and integrates to 1. We define $\mathcal{R}(x)$ to be constant in the region of interest, making

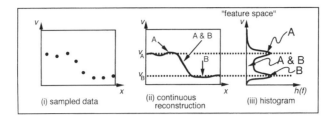

Figure 7.5 Histogram calculation. The scalar samples in (i) are measurements from a dataset containing two materials, A and B. One material has measurement values near v_A and the other near v_B. In (ii) we reconstruct a continuous function from those samples, with relatively flat regions at the two material values. These flat regions correspond to the Gaussian-shaped peaks centered around v_A and v_B in the histogram, (iii), which is shown on its side to emphasize the axis that it shares with the spatial data.

every spatial point contribute equally to the histogram $h^{\mathcal{R}}(v)$. Note also that $h^{\mathcal{R}}(v)$ integrates to 1. δ is the Dirac-delta function. Figure 7.5 shows an example of calculating a normalized histogram from a continuous function.

We use equation (7.1) both as a starting point for deriving histogram basis functions and also for calculating histograms of regions of our datasets.

7.2.2   Construction of a New Bayesian Classification Algorithm

Construction of a new classification algorithm involves four steps: choosing voxel-info to represent the information in a voxel, selecting a set of assumptions about the collection process, defining a parameterized model of the voxel-info, and deriving material probability estimates.

Choose voxel-info.   Our algorithms use histograms calculated over the region of a voxel as voxel-info; other choices are possible. We have chosen histograms for a number of reasons. First, they generalize single measurements to measurements over a region, so classification concepts that apply to single measurements generalize. Second, the histograms can be calculated easily. Third, the histograms capture information about neighboring voxels, which increases the information content of the voxel-info and improves the classification results. Fourth, histograms are orientation-independent; orientation independence reduces the number of parameters in the classification process, hence simplifying and accelerating it.

As with many other techniques, ours works on vector valued volume data, in which each material has a characteristic vector value rather than a characteristic scalar value. Vector valued datasets have a number of advantages and generally give better classification results. First, they have an improved signal-to-noise ratio. Second, they frequently distinguish similar materials more effectively (see Figure 7.6). The jump from scalar to two-valued vector data is the most significant. In scalar valued datasets it is difficult to distinguish a mixture of two pure materials with values v_A and v_B from a pure material with some intermediate value such as $v_C = (v_A + v_B)/2$. This is because all three material values are collinear, as they must be for such a dataset. With more measurement dimensions in the dataset, collinearity is less frequent for

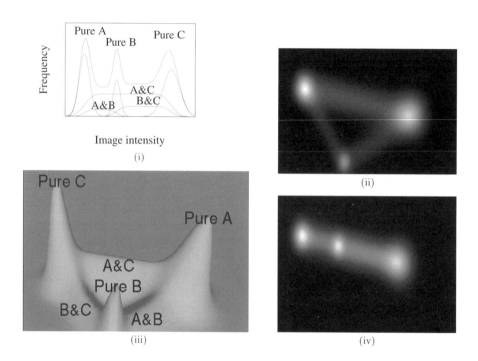

Figure 7.6 Benefits of histograms of vector valued data. We show histograms of an object with three materials. (i) is a histogram of scalar data and shows that material mean values are collinear; therefore, distinguishing among more than two materials is often ambiguous. (ii) represents a histogram of vector-valued data, with one MRI value along the axes at the bottom of the figure and one along the left side. Brighter points represent larger values of the histogram. (iii) is another representation of the same histogram. The histogram shows that mean values often move away from collinearity in higher dimensions. (iv) shows a different histogram demonstrating that the collinearity problem can occur with vector valued data. (See also color Plate 26)

most combinations of three or more materials, although Figure 7.6(iv) (Plate 26) illustrates that it can still occur. When it does occur, the classification works as for scalar valued data.

Codify collection assumptions. In the second step we codify a set of assumptions about the data collection process. The assumptions embody information about:

- how sampling works on the machine we are using
- the responses of materials or combinations of materials to the measurement process
- the spatial uniformity of the measurements
- geometric characteristics of our objects

For our example we will assume that there is a known discrete set of materials, that measurements for a single material are distributed normally, and that each voxel consists of exactly one material. Section 7.3 lists the assumptions for our algorithms, some of which are illustrated in Figure 7.7 (Plate 27).

Model voxel-info. From our choice of voxel-info and the set of assumptions about the data collection process, we define a parameterized model of the voxel-info, $f(\alpha)$. The parameters, α, for the voxel-info model are divided into two classes. The first, *dataset parameters*, consists of those that are known before the voxel classification process. The second, *voxel parameters*, vary from voxel to voxel and are estimated as the result of the classification process.

For our example the dataset parameters are a mean and deviation for measurements of each material; the single voxel parameter is discrete-valued and each value corresponds to one of the possible materials.

Estimate material probabilities. Given voxel-info, h, which encodes information from a single voxel and a parameterized model of the voxel-info, $f(\alpha)$, we want to find the most likely set of parameters α. The *posterior probability* defines how likely a set of parameters α is given an observed voxel-info, h:

$$P(\alpha|h) \tag{7.2}$$

By maximizing the posterior probability we find the most likely set of parameters. Equation (7.2) cannot, in general, be calculated directly, so we use Bayes' Theorem to decompose it into pieces that we can either calculate directly or estimate.

$$P(\alpha|h) = \frac{P(\alpha)P(h|\alpha)}{P(h)} \tag{7.3}$$

$P(h|\alpha)$ is the *likelihood* of a particular instance of voxel-info for a given set of voxel parameters. We calculate it by comparing the parameterized model of the voxel-info to the actual voxel-info and quantifying the difference.

$P(\alpha)$ is the *prior probability* and tells us how likely each set of parameters is. We estimate the prior probability from the model of the voxel-info and from the assumptions that we make about the data collection process.

$P(h)$ is the *global likelihood* of a particular instance of voxel-info. We assume that it is a constant function of h. It becomes a normalization factor for equation (7.3).

7.2.3   Classification

Estimate dataset parameters.   Any dataset parameters must be estimated before the classifier can be used. We estimate them by calculating their values for a training set of voxels with known voxel parameters. In our example we would calculate the mean and variance of a set of measurements known to be from each discrete material.

Classify voxels.   Finally, we calculate the voxel-info, h, for each voxel and use the classifier to estimate the voxel parameters.

7.2.4   Example of Classification Algorithm Construction

In this section we construct the Bayesian classifier for the example we introduced in Section 7.2.2. This classifier is not new [DH73], but its construction within our framework illustrates how to create a classifier.

Example voxel-info.   For our example we define voxel-info h_e as the single data measurement at the center of a voxel.

Example assumptions.

e_1: Each measurement comes from exactly one material
e_2: The measurements from each material are normally distributed
e_3: We know the number of materials and can identify samples from each material within the data
e_4: All materials are equally likely

Example model of voxel-info.   Our model of the voxel data, $f_e(\alpha_e)$, has a single discrete voxel parameter, α_e, that specifies the material within the voxel.

$$f_e(\alpha_e) = \mu_{\alpha_e} \tag{7.4}$$

For each material i, our model has two dataset parameters, μ_i and σ_i, defining the expected value and the standard deviation of measurements.

Example material probabilities.   From assumptions e_1 and e_2, the likelihood, $P(h_e|\alpha_e)$, can be calculated by evaluating a normal distribution with mean μ_{α_e} and variance $\sigma_{\alpha_e}^2$:
From assumption e_4, the prior probability, $P_e(\alpha_e)$, is $\frac{1}{n_m}$ where n_m is the number of materials.

Example dataset parameter estimation.   The dataset parameters consist of the mean and variance of measurements of each discrete material. From assumption e_3 we find the dataset parameters by interactively selecting a set of points in the dataset for each material. We define each set as measurements of the single material they represent; from them we calculate the mean and variance for each material.

Example classification. We iterate over each voxel calculating the most likely value for the single voxel parameter, α_e; for each voxel we measure h_e, the value at the center of the voxel. For each possible material we calculate the corresponding posterior probability, $P(\alpha_e | h_e)$, and choose the largest of these values. This gives us the most likely material.

7.3   A FAMILY OF SOLUTIONS

In this section we give an overview of three new classification algorithms constructed within our framework and compare and contrast them with one another. We first list the assumptions that are common to all three algorithms and the dataset parameters that these assumptions imply. We then present the assumptions unique to each algorithm and summarize both the dataset and voxel parameters.

7.3.1   Assumptions Common to New Algorithms

We make several assumptions that are consistent among the new algorithms that we have developed. Each algorithm also makes additional assumptions detailed in subsequent sections.

e_{c1}: **Discrete materials.** The first assumption is that materials within the objects that we measure are discrete at the resolution that we are sampling. Material boundaries are not assumed to be aligned with the sampling grid. We make this assumption because we are generally looking for boundaries between materials, and because we are starting from sampled data, which loses information about detail that is finer than the sampling rate.

    This assumption does not preclude homogeneous combinations of sub-materials that can be treated as a single material at our sampling resolution. For example, muscle may contain some water, and yet be treated as a separate material from water. This assumption is not satisfied where materials gradually transition from one to another over many samples or are not relatively uniformly mixed. Section 7.5 discusses cases where this assumption is not satisfied.

e_{c2}: **Normally distributed noise.** The second assumption is that noise is added to each discrete sample and that the noise is normally distributed. We assume a different variance in the noise for each material. This assumption is not strictly satisfied for MRI data in some cases, but seems to be satisfied sufficiently to classify data well.

e_{c3}: **Data satisfies sampling theorem.** The third assumption we make is that the sampled datasets we classify satisfy the sampling theorem [OWY83]. The sampling theorem states that if we sample a sufficiently band-limited function, we can exactly reconstruct that function from the samples.

    From assumption e_{c1} the underlying physical object has discontinuous boundaries between materials, and an infinite-precision MRI machine would generate a dataset with discontinuities at material boundaries. At finite resolutions, the measurement function must be band limited so that it can be reconstructed from the samples. MRI slice data generally satisfies this assumption or can be prepro-

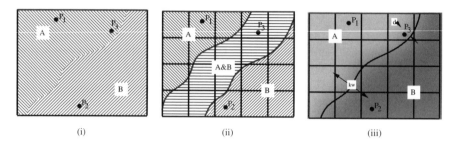

(i)   (ii)   (iii)

Figure 7.7 The three classification algorithms start from the assumption that in a real-world object each point is exactly one material, as in (i). The measurement process creates samples that mix materials together, from which we reconstruct a continuous, band-limited measurement function $\rho(x)$. For some values of x, e.g., P_1 and P_2, $\rho(x)$ returns the signature of a pure material. For other values of x, e.g., P_3, $\rho(x)$ returns a combination of the pure material signatures. Algorithm A, (ii), models the measurements as a linear combination of pure material signatures and signatures of mixtures of pairs of materials. Two-material mixing occurs in the region labeled "A & B," and each voxel (delimited by grid lines) can contain some of each signature. Algorithms B and C, (iii), use a parametric model that is based on the distance from a voxel to a boundary between materials. The grid lines surround voxels. (See also color Plate 27)

cessed to satisfy it [Lai92], [GLS⁺97] within the slice. Without data that satisfy the sampling theorem, we cannot reconstruct a continuous function, and without a continuous function, we cannot extract geometric models as shown in Section 7.4.

7.3.2   Overview of Algorithm A: Partial-volume Mixtures

Our new partial-volume mixtures algorithm was developed to create classified data with fewer boundary artifacts so that we could produce better geometric models. The choice of voxel-info, the model of the voxel-info, and some of the assumptions are formulated to capture and identify information about the boundaries. The remainder of the assumptions help make some of the probability calculations more tractable.

We assume, as in Figure 7.7(i) (Plate 27), that each voxel is a mixture of materials, with mixtures like "A & B" occurring where the band-limiting effects of the data collection process blur pure materials together, as in Figure 7.7(ii) (Plate 27). From this assumption we derive basis functions that model histograms for pure materials and for mixtures of two materials.

Additions to common assumptions.

e_{m4}: **Linear mixtures.** Each voxel measurement is a linear combination of pure material measurements and measurements of their pairwise mixtures.

e_{m5}: **Uniform tissue measurements.** Measurements for the same material have the same expected value throughout a dataset.

e_{m6}: **Box filtering.** The spatial measurement process can be approximated by a box filter for the purpose of calculating histogram basis functions.

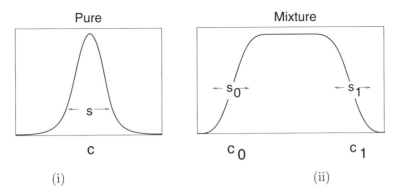

Figure 7.8   Dataset parameters for a pure material histogram basis function, shown in (i), include c, the mean value for the material, and s, which measures the standard deviation of measurements (see Equation 7.6). (ii) shows corresponding parameters for a two-material mixture basis function.

e_{m7}: **Materials identifiable in histogram of entire dataset.** The signatures for each material and mixture must be identifiable in a histogram of the entire dataset.

Description.   The parameters for each voxel in this algorithm are density values for each pure material and for each pairwise combination of materials, and an estimate of the low-frequency noise within the voxel. The densities sum to one, and each density weights a histogram basis function for either a pure material or a mixture. The basis function for pure materials is a normal distribution.

$$P_e(h_e | \alpha_e) = \frac{1}{\sigma_{\alpha_e} \sqrt{2\pi}} \exp\left(-\frac{1}{2} \left(\frac{\alpha_e - \mu_{\alpha_e}}{\sigma_{\alpha_e}} \right)^2 \right) \tag{7.5}$$

$$f_{\text{single}}(v; c, s) = \prod_{i=1}^{n_v} \frac{1}{s_i \sqrt{2\pi}} \exp\left(-\frac{1}{2} \left(\frac{v_i - c_i}{s_i} \right)^2 \right) \tag{7.6}$$

The basis function for a mixture is

$$f_{\text{double}}(v; c, s) = \int_0^1 f_{\text{single}}(v; (1 - t)c_1 + tc_2, s) dt. \tag{7.7}$$

Both basis functions are shown in Figure 7.8.

   The dataset parameters are the mean, c, and standard deviation, s, for each pure material, as well as an expected deviation of the model histogram from actual histograms. The parameters are estimated by analyzing a histogram taken over the entire dataset and fitting a combination of materials to that histogram.

7.3.3   Overview of Algorithm B: Boundary Distance

The boundary distance algorithm addresses some of the limitations we discovered in the partial volume mixtures algorithm. The voxel-info and most of the assumptions are the same, but the histogram basis functions differ. The main change is that the distance from a boundary is explicitly incorporated into the histogram basis function for mixtures, as shown in Figure 7.7(iii) (Plate 27). The explicit model better fits histograms of voxels near boundaries. A second change is that the histogram basis functions are derived with the more accurate assumption of Gaussian filtering.

Additions to common assumptions

e_{b4}: **Only pairwise mixtures.** Each voxel measurement is of either a pure material or a mixture of exactly two materials near a boundary.

e_{b5}: **Uniform tissue measurements.** Measurements for the same material have the same expected value throughout a dataset.

e_{b6}: **Gaussian filtering.** The measurement process can be approximated by a Gaussian filter for the purpose of calculating histogram basis functions.

e_{b7}: **Known materials.** We know the number of materials and can identify samples from each material and mixture within the data.

Description.   The voxel parameters for this algorithm are a discrete parameter, α_b, that determines the material or mixture, a signed distance, d, from a boundary for mixtures, and an estimate, $\bar{N}$, of the low-frequency noise within the voxel. Once again, the histogram basis functions for pure materials are normal distributions. The basis functions for mixtures are

$$
\begin{aligned}
f_{\text{boundary}}(v; d, \bar{N}, c, s, k_w) = \\
k_n(v; s) * \left(\left(H(d + \tfrac{k_h}{2} - \tfrac{k_e(v)}{k_w}) - H(d - \tfrac{k_h}{2} - \tfrac{k_e(v)}{k_w}) \right) \left| \tfrac{e^{k_e(v)}\sqrt{\pi}}{(c_2 - c_1)k_w} \right| \right)
\end{aligned}
\tag{7.8}
$$

where $k_e(v) = \text{erf}^{-1}(\frac{c_1 + c_2 - 2v}{c_1 - c_2})$ and $H(x)$ is the Heaviside, or step, function. The basis functions are shown in Figure 7.9 and 7.10.

The dataset parameters are the mean, c, and standard deviation, s, values for each pure material, the width, k_w (in samples), of the acquisition sampling kernel, and an expected deviation of the model histogram from actual histograms. They are estimated from a training set of points interactively chosen for each material and mixture.

7.3.4   Overview of Algorithm C: Boundary Distance with Nonuniform Material Signatures

Our third algorithm augments the boundary distance algorithm to handle a common characteristic of MRI data that often complicates classification: MRI measurements of the same material can be different at different spatial locations. There are a number of factors that can cause these intensity distortions, from antenna coils that produce spatially dependent RF radiation to different amounts of RF absorption in different parts of an object being imaged. The algorithm relaxes the assumption that the expected value for a material is constant; instead, the expected value is a function of spatial location.

Additions to common assumptions.   Only e_{v5} differs from the assumptions for the boundary distance algorithm.

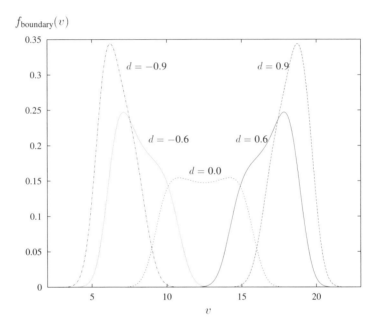

Figure 7.9   Histogram basis functions, $f_{\mathrm{boundary}}(v)$, for scalar data. The shapes approach normal distributions as d, the distance from the boundary to a voxel center, moves away from 0.

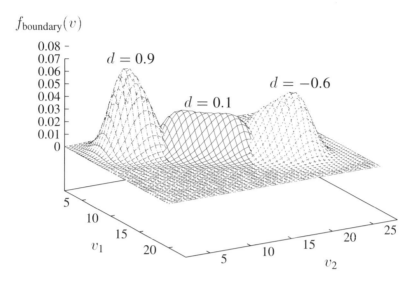

$f_{\text{boundary}}(v)$

Figure 7.10   Histogram basis functions, $f_{\text{boundary}}(v)$, for vector valued data. Three different values of d, the distance from the boundary to a voxel center, are represented.

e_{v4}: **Only pairwise mixtures.**

e_{v5}: **Predictable tissue measurements.** Measurements for the same material have an expected value that can be modeled with a small number of parameters across a dataset.

e_{v6}: **Gaussian filtering.**

e_{v7}: **Known materials.**

Description.   This algorithm is very similar to the boundary distance algorithm. The basis functions and voxel parameters are the same. Only the dataset parameters that determine the expected value for a tissue measurement are different. In this case, the expected value is a parameterized function of space. Its parameters are calculated from a set of interactively-specified points for each material. The calculation is similar to calculating a mean and variance from a set of points, but the mean is now a function of spatial location.

7.4   RESULTS

We have applied our new technique to several MRI datasets, both simulated and real. Figure 7.11 shows results generated from simulated imaging data of a tennis ball-like object – a hollow ball with two concentric surface layers. Figures 7.3 and 7.12 (see Plate 28) show classification results from an MRI section of a human brain.

   We first compare our techniques with a probabilistic approach that uses pure materials only and only a single measurement value per voxel. The new technique produces

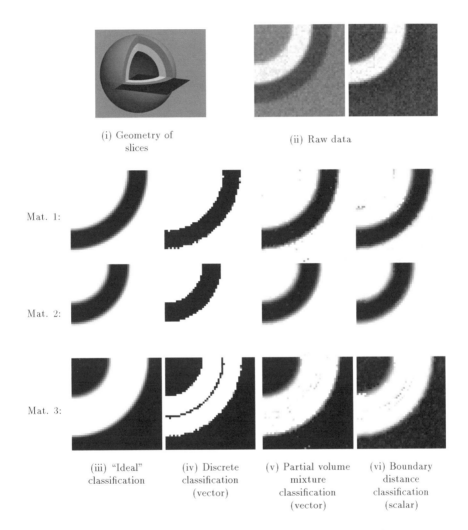

Figure 7.11 (i) Geometry of slices (ii) Raw data

Mat. 1:

Mat. 2:

Mat. 3:

(iii) "Ideal" classification (iv) Discrete classification (vector) (v) Partial volume mixture classification (vector) (vi) Boundary distance classification (scalar)

Figure 7.11 The partial-volume, boundary distance, and discrete algorithms are compared in classifying simulated MRI data. (ii) shows the simulated data, which contains three different materials. The geometry that the data measures is shown in (i). (iii) shows what an "ideal" classification algorithm should produce and (iv)–(vi) show results from different algorithms. Note that the new algorithms (v) and (vi) produce results most similar to the ideal case, and that (vi) does so even with scalar data.

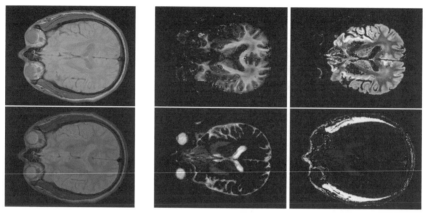

(i) Original Data

(ii) Results of Algorithm
Classified White Matter, Gray Matter
Cerebro-Spinal Fluid, Muscle

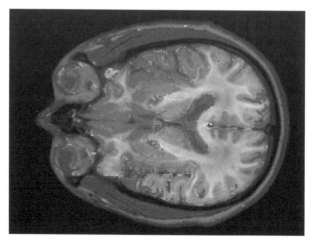

(iii) Combined Classified Image

Figure 7.12   One slice of data from a human brain. (i) shows the original two-valued data, (ii) shows four of the identified materials, white matter, gray matter, cerebro-spinal fluid, and muscle, separated out into different images, and (iii) shows the results of the new classification mapped to different colors. Note the smooth boundaries where materials meet and the much lower incidence of misclassified samples than in Figure 7.3. (See also color Plate 28)

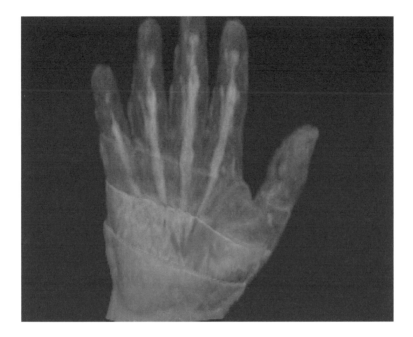

Figure 7.13 A volume rendering image of a human hand dataset. The opacity of different materials is decreased above cutting planes to show details of the classification process within the hand. (See also color Plate 29)

many fewer misclassified voxels, particularly in regions where materials are mixed due to filtering. The difference is illustrated in Figures 7.11(iii) and (iv) where an incorrect layer of background material has been introduced between the white and gray regions. This layer occurs because multiple materials are present in each voxel. The simulated data that we classified is shown in Figure 7.11(ii) with Figure 7.11(iii) illustrating what an ideal classification algorithm would produce. Discrete classification, using vector data, but only a single measurement point per voxel and assuming only pure materials, produces the results in Figure 7.11(iv). Note the jaggy edges and the band of misclassified data for material 3 along the boundary between materials 1 and 2. Figure 7.11(v) and Figure 7.11(vi) show the partial volume mixtures algorithm and the boundary distance algorithm. Even with scalar data the boundary distance algorithm achieves results very close to the ideal case.

Figure 7.3 and 7.12(iii) (see Plate 28) also show comparative results for classification of an MR section through a human brain. Note in the new classification results the reduction of jagged edges between materials and the virtual elimination of the layer of misclassified brain material just under the skin.

Models and volume rendered images, as shown in Figure 7.13 (Plate 29) and Figure 7.14 (Plate 30), benefit from our approach because less incorrect information is introduced into the classified datasets, and so the images and models more accurately depict the objects they are representing. With other classification techniques, models and images contain jaggy artifacts, particularly along surfaces where materials meet, because the algorithms are less accurate there.

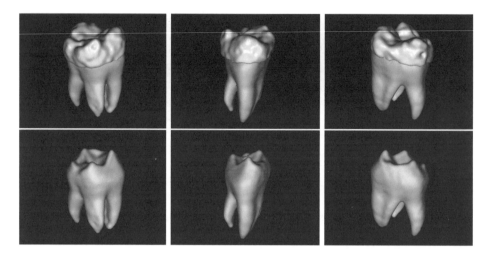

Figure 7.14 A geometric model of tooth dentine and enamel created by collecting MRI data using a technique that images hard solid materials [GLF+95] and classifying dentine and enamel in the volume data with our new partial-volume mixtures algorithm. Polygonal isosurfaces define the bounding surfaces of the dentine and enamel. The enamel–dentine boundary, shown in the lower images, is difficult to examine noninvasively using any other technique. (See also color Plate 30)

7.5   DISCUSSION

We have made several assumptions and approximations while developing and implementing the continuous Bayesian algorithms. This section discusses some of the trade-offs and suggests some possible directions for future work.

7.5.1   Mixtures of Three or More Materials

We assume that each measurement contains values from at most two materials, although the approach easily extends to mixtures with more materials. We chose two-material mixtures because surfaces between boundaries of pure materials are one of the most important parts of computer graphics models. Voxels containing three-material mixtures happen near lines where three materials meet, and are generally much less common because the dimensionality of the lines is smaller than the dimensionality of surfaces where two materials meet.

Our algorithm chooses a classification for voxels containing more than two materials from the set of two-material mixtures. Generally, the two most prevalent materials in the voxel influence the choice, producing a dataset with small artifacts where three or more materials come together.

7.5.2   More Sophisticated Geometric Basis Functions

The basis functions that we have developed model the two most common geometric cases: samples within regions of pure material and samples near surface boundaries. Additional basis functions, however, could model other geometries and create more accurate models. Examples include samples near edges where three materials come together, or points near membranes that are thinner than the sample spacing, where, again, three materials would have an effect on the measurement.

7.5.3   Ambiguous Classification

For a voxel that is well within a region of pure material A, the algorithms sometimes correctly classify the voxel as pure material A, and sometimes classify it as a mixture of A and a small amount of some other material. Both solutions are physically reasonable because the mixture basis functions approach a normal distribution as the boundary distance parameter d moves away from zero.

Similarly, two different mixtures, each containing material A, can match a voxel that is within a region of pure material A. Again, the choice is not critical.

7.5.4   Sensitivity to Interactively Selected Material Classes

The results of the algorithm are highly dependent on the material points selected interactively to represent each pure material and each pair of materials. These points must be selected carefully, and should come from a set of points that actually represent a single consistent material. Representing points from two materials as one material can create a situation where the distributions of the sample values do not match a normal distribution, and the classification results are less accurate.

7.5.5   Sensitivity to Contrast Between Materials

The classification is sensitive to the contrast-to-noise ratio between different materials. If this ratio is too small, materials cannot be distinguished effectively. We pass this requirement back to the data acquisition process, and use goal-directed techniques to ensure that we collect data that can be classified effectively [LBJ97].

7.5.6   Computational Expense

The implementations described in this chapter are computationally expensive. The optimization process must be run on each voxel in a dataset. At ten voxels per second, a medium-sized dataset of $256 \times 256 \times 64$ voxels runs in about five days. Through approximations it may be possible to reduce this time significantly.

The algorithm processes each voxel independently, and so is highly amenable to a domain-decomposition parallel solution. In fact, we have run it on a network of ten HP 9000/700 and DEC Alpha workstations and gotten a speedup of almost ten in classifying medium to large datasets.

7.5.7   Incorporating Additional Global Information

Except for the interpolation of samples, we currently classify each voxel without regard to its neighbors and without directly using the interactively selected representative points for each material. Both types of information could be incorporated into the prior probability estimates to influence the classification process.

7.6   CONCLUSIONS

The algorithms described here for classifying scalar and vector valued volume data produces more accurate results than existing techniques in many cases, particularly at boundaries between materials. The aspects responsible for this improvement are: 1) the reconstruction of a continuous function from the samples, 2) the use of histograms taken over voxel-sized regions to represent the contents of the voxels, 3) the modeling of sub-voxel partial-volume effects caused by the band-limiting nature of the acquisition process, and 4) the use of a Bayesian classification approach. We have demonstrated the technique on both simulated and real data, and it correctly classifies many voxels containing multiple materials.

The construction of a continuous function is based on the sampling theorem, and while it does not introduce new information, it provides a richer context for the information that classification algorithms such as ours can use. It incorporates information about neighboring samples into the classification process for a voxel in a natural and mathematically rigorous way and thereby greatly increases classification accuracy. In addition, because the operations that can be safely performed directly on sampled data are so limited, treating the data as a continuous function helps to avoid introducing artifacts.

Histograms are a natural choice for representing voxel contents for a number of reasons. First, they generalize single measurements to measurements over a region, allowing classification concepts that apply to single measurements to generalize. Second, the histograms can be calculated easily. Third, the histograms capture information about neighboring voxels; this increases the information content over single measurements and improves classification results. Fourth, histograms are orientation-independent; orientation independence reduces the number of parameters in the classification process, hence simplifying and accelerating it.

Partial-volume effects are a nemesis of classification algorithms, which traditionally have drawn from techniques that classify isolated measurements. These techniques do not take into account the related nature of spatially correlated measurements. Many attempts have been made to model partial-volume effects, and ours continues that trend, with results that suggest that further study is warranted.

We believe that the Bayesian approach we describe is a useful formalism for capturing the assumptions and information gleaned from the continuous representation of the sample values, the histograms calculated from them, and the partial-volume effects of imaging. Together, these allow a generalization of many sample-based classification techniques, three of which we have demonstrated.

ACKNOWLEDGMENTS

This work was supported in part by grants from Apple, DEC, Hewlett Packard, and IBM. Additional support was provided by NSF (ASC-89-20219) as part of the NSF STC for Computer Graphics and Scientific Visualization, by the DOE (DE-FG03-92ER25134) as part of the Center for Research in Computational Biology, and by the National Institute on Drug Abuse, the National Institute of Mental Health, and the National Science Foundation as part of the Human Brain Project.

Thanks to Al Barr for much advice, to Kurt Fleischer for his help in developing Algorithm A, to Matt Avalos for extensive programming support, to Jim Arvo, Al Barr, and Peter Schröder for brainstorming on Figure 7.1, and to Pratik Ghosh and Russ Jacobs for the collaborative effort behind Figure 7.14 (Plate 30).

References

[ABSS94]   V. Anupam, C. L. Bajaj, D. R. Schikore, and M. Schikore. Distributed and collaborative visualization. *Computer*, 27(7):37–43, July 1994.

[AFH80]   E. Artzy, G. Frieder, and G. T. Herman. The theory, design, implementation and evaluation of a three-dimensional surface detection algorithm. In *Computer Graphics (SIGGRAPH '80 Proceedings)*, volume 14, pages 2–9, 1980.

[AGS95]   A. B. Amin, A. Grama, and V. Singh. Fast volume rendering using an efficient, scalable parallel formulation of the shear-warp algorithm. In *Proceedings 1995 Parallel Rendering Symposium*, pages 7–14, Atlanta, GA, October 1995.

[ASK92]   R. Avila, L. M. Sobierajski, and A. E. Kaufman. Towards a comprehensive volume visualization systems. In *Proceedings Visualization '92*, pages 13–20, Boston, MA, October 1992.

[Baj88]   C. Bajaj. Geometric modeling with algebraic surfaces. In D. Handscomb, editor, *The Mathematics of Surfaces III*, pages 3–48. Oxford Univ. Press, 1988.

[Ban94]   D. C. Banks. Illumination in diverse co-dimensions. In *SIGGRAPH '94*, Orlando, FL, 1994. ACM SIGGRAPH.

[BBB+97]   J. Bloomenthal, C. L. Bajaj, J. Blinn, M.-P. Cani-Gascuel, A. Rockwood, B. Wyvill, and G. Wyvill. *Introduction to Implicit Surfaces*. Morgan Kaufman Publishers, 1997.

[BBX95]   C. L. Bajaj, F. Bernardini, and G. Xu. Automatic reconstruction of surfaces and scalar fields from 3D scans. In R. Cook, editor, *SIGGRAPH 95 Conference Proceedings*, Annual Conference Series, pages 109–118. ACM SIGGRAPH, Addison Wesley, August 1995. Held in Los Angeles, California, 06-11 August 1995.

[BC94]   K.-P. Beier and Y. Chen. Highlight-line algorithm for realtime surface quality assessment. *CAD*, 26(4):268–277, 1994.

[BCL96a]   C. L. Bajaj, E. J. Coyle, and K.-N. Lin. Surface and 3D triangular meshes from planar cross sections. In *Proc. of the 5th International Meshing Roundtable*, number SAND96-2301 UC-405 in Sandia Report, pages 169–178, 1996.

[BCL96b]   C. L. Bajaj, E. J. Coyle, and K.-N. Lin. Arbitrary topology shape reconstruction from planar cross sections. *Graphical Models and Image Processing*, 6(58):524–543, November 1996.

[Bei87]   K.-P. Beier. The porcupine technique: Principles, applications, and algorithms. Technical report, University of Michigan, October 1987.

[BFFH88]   R. Barnhill, G. Farin, L. Fayard, and H. Hagen. Twists, curvature and surface interrogation. *CAD 20*, pages 314–346, 1988.

[BFGS86]   L. Bergman, H. Fuchs, E. Grant, and S. Spach. Image rendering by adaptive refinement. *Computer Graphics*, 20(4):29–37, August 1986.

[BFH86]   J. Beck, R. Farouki, and J. Hinds. Surface analysis methods. *IEEE CG & Appl.*, 6:19–35, 1986.

[BFK84]   W. Boehm, G. Farin, and J. Kahmann. A survey of curve and surface methods in CAGD. *Computer Aided Geometric Design*, 1(1):1–60, 1984.

[BHR+94]   M. Brill, H. Hagen, H.-C. Rodrian, W. Djatschin, and S. V. Klimenko. Streamball techniques for flow vizualization. In R. D. Bergeron and A. E. Kaufman, editors, *Proceedings of the Conference on Visualization*, pages 225–231, Los Alamitos, CA, USA, October 1994. IEEE Computer Society Press.

[BLM95]   G. G. Becker, D. A. Lane, and N. L. Max. Unsteady flow volumes. In *Visualization '95*, Atlanta, GA, 1995. IEEE Computer Society Press.

[BLM97]   M. J. Bentum, B. B. A. Lichtenbelt, and T. Malzbender. Frequency analysis of gradient estimators in volume rendering. *IEEE Transactions on Visualization Computer Graphics*, 1997.

[BLMP97]   C. Bajaj, H. Y. Lee, R. Merkert, and V. Pascucci. NURBS based B-rep models for macromolecules and their properties. In C. Hoffmann and W. Bronsvort, editors, *Proceedings of the 4th Symposium on Solid Modeling and Applications*, pages 217–228, New York, May 14–16 1997. ACM Press.

[Boe93]   W. Boehm. *Curves and Surfaces for Computer Aided Geometric Design*, chapters 11 & 22: Differential Geometry I & II. Academic Press, Boston, 3rd edition, 1993.

[BOP92]   R. Barnhill, K. Opitz, and H. Pottmann. Fat surfaces: a trivariate approach to triangle-based interpolation on surfaces. *Computer Aided Geometric Design*, 9:365–378, 1992.

[Bow95]   J. E. Bowie, editor. *Data Visualization in Molecular Science*. Addison-Wesley Publishing Company, 1995.

[BPS96]   C. L. Bajaj, V. Pascucci, and D. R. Schikore. Fast isocontouring for improved interactivity. In *Proceedings of 1996 Symposium on Volume Visualization*, pages 39–46, October 1996.

[BPS97a]   C. L. Bajaj, V. Pascucci, and D. R. Schikore. The contour spectrum. In *Proceedings of IEEE Visualization '97*, pages 167–173, October 1997.

[BPS97b]   C. L. Bajaj, V. Pascucci, and D. R. Schikore. Fast isocontouring for structured and unstructured meshes in any dimension. In *Proceedings of Late Breaking Hot Topics (IEEE Visualization 1997)*, pages 25–28, October 1997.

[BR94]   C. Bajaj and A. Royappa. *Triangulation and Display of Arbitrary Rational Parametric Surfaces*. In R. Bergeron and A. Kaufman, editors, Proc. of IEEE Visualization '94 Conference, 1994.

[BS94]   D. C. Banks and B. A. Singer. Vortex tubes in turbulent flows: Identification, representation, reconstruction. In *Visualization '94*, pages 132–139, Washington, DC, 1994. IEEE Computer Society Press.

[BS95]   C. L. Bajaj and D. R. Schikore. Decimation of 2d scalar data with error control, 1995. Purdue University, Computer Science Technical Report, CSD-TR-95-005.

[BS96a]   C. L. Bajaj and D. R. Schikore. Error-bounded reduction of triangle meshes with multivariate data. In *Proceedings of SPIE Symposium on Visual Data Exploration and Analysis III*, 1996.

[BS96b]   C. L. Bajaj, V, Pascucci and D. R. Schikore. Visualization of scalar topology for structural enhancement. In *Proceedings of IEEE Visualization '98*, pages 51–58, 1996.

[BS97]   C. L. Bajaj and D. R. Schikore. Topology preserving data simplification with error bounds, 1997.

[BX94]   C. Bajaj and G. Xu. Modeling Scattered Function Data on Curved Surface. In J. Chen, N. Thalmann, Z. Tang, and D. Thalmann, editors, *Fundamentals of Computer Graphics*, pages 19–29, Beijing, China, 1994.

[CA91]   R. Crawfis and M. Allison. A scientific visualization synthesizer. In *Visualization '91*, San Diego, CA, 1991. IEEE Computer Society Press.

[Cat74]   E. Catmull. *A subdivision for computer display of curved surfaces*. PhD thesis, University of Utah, 1974.

[CCF94]   B. Cabral, N. Cam, and J. Foran. Accelerated volume rendering and tomographic reconstruction using texture mapping hardware. In *Proceedings, 1994 Symposium on Volume Visualization, IEEE Computer Society Press*, Los Alamifos, CA, 1994.

[CDM$^+$94] P. Cignoni, L. De Floriani, C. Montoni, E. Puppo, and R. Scopigno. Multiresolution modeling and visualization of volume data based on simplicial complexes.

In A. Kaufman and W. Krueger, editors, *1994 Symposium on Volume Visualization*, pages 19–26. ACM SIGGRAPH, October 1994.

[CHK91]   H. S. Choi, D. R. Haynor, and Y. M. Kim. Partial volume tissue classification of multichannel magnetic resonance images — A mixel model. *IEEE Transactions on Medical Images*, 10(3):395–407, 1991.

[CL93]   B. Cabral and L. Leedom. Imaging vector fields using line integral convolution. *Computer Graphics*, 27(Annual Conference Series):263–270, 1993.

[Cle93]   W. S. Cleveland. *Visualizing Data*. Hobart Press, Summit, New Jersey, 1993.

[CLKJ90]   H. E. Cline, W. E. Lorensen, R. Kikinis, and F. Jolesz. Three-dimensional segmentation of MR images of the head using probability and connectivity. *Journal of Computer Assisted Tomography*, 14(6):1037–1045, 1990.

[CM92a]   B. Corrie and P. Mackerras. Parallel volume rendering and data coherence on the Fujitsu AP100. Technical Report TR-CS-92-11, Department of Computer Science, Australian National University, Canberra, ACT, Australia, 1992.

[CM92b]   R. Crawfis and N. Max. Direct volume visualization of three-dimensional vector fields. In *Proceedings of the 1992 Workshop on Volume Visualization*, New York, 1992. ACM SIGGRAPH.

[CM93]   R. Crawfis and N. Max. Texture splats for 3D vector and scalar field visualization. In *Visualization '93*, San Jose, CA, 1993. IEEE Computer Society Press.

[CMPS97]   P. Cignoni, C. Montani, E. Puppo, and R. Scopigno. Speeding up isosurface extraction using interval trees. *IEEE Transactions on Visualization and Computer Graphics*, 3(2):158–170, 1997.

[COL96]   D. Cohen-Or and Y. Levanoni. Temporal continuity in levels of detail. In R. Yagel and G. M. Nielson, editors, *Visualization '96 Proceedings*, pages 37–42, 1996.

[CPD+96]   A. Certain, J. Popović, T. DeRose, T. Duchamp, D. Salesin, and W. Stuetzle. Interactive multiresolution surface viewing. In H. Rushmeier, editor, *SIGGRAPH 96 Conference Proceedings*, Annual Conference Series, pages 91–98. ACM SIGGRAPH, Addison Wesley, August 1996. Held in New Orleans, Louisiana, 04-09 August 1996.

[Cra95]   R. Crawfis. *New techniques for the scientific visualization of three-dimensional multi-variate and vector fields*. PhD thesis, University of California, Davis, 1995.

[CS93]   D. Cohen and Z. Shefer. Proximity clouds – an acceleration technique for 3D grid traversal. Technical Report FC 93-01, Ben Gurion University of the Negev, February 1993.

[CS97]   Y.-J. Chiang and C. T. Silva. I/o optimal isosurface extraction. In *Proceedings of IEEE Visualization '97*, pages 293–300, October 1997.

[CU92]   G. G. Cameron and P. E. Underill. Rendering volumetric medical image data on a SIMD architecture computer. In *Proceedings of Third Eurographics Workshop on Rendering*, pages 135–145, Bristol, UK, May 1992.

[CVC+95]   L. P. Clarke, R. P. Velthuizen, M. A. Camacho, J. J. Neine, M. Vaidyanathan, L. O. Hall, R. W. Thatcher, and M. L. Silbiger. MRI segmentation: Methods and applications. *Magnetic Resonance Imaging*, 13(3):343–368, 1995.

[CVM+96]   J. Cohen, A. Varshney, D. Manocha, G. Turk, H. Weber, P. Agarwal, Frederick P. Brooks, Jr., and W. Wright. Simplification envelopes. In H. Rushmeier, editor, *SIGGRAPH '96 Conference Proceedings*, Annual Conference Series, pages 119–128, 1996. Held in New Orleans, LA, August 4-9, 1996.

[Dar96]   G. Darboux. *Leçons sur la théorie générale des surfaces*, volume tome 4. Gauthier-Villars, Paris, France, 1896.

[Dau92]   I. Daubechies. *Ten Lectures on Wavelets*, volume 61 of *CBMS-NSF Regional Conference Series in Applied Mathematics*. Society for Industrial and Applied Mathematics, Philadelphia, 1992.

[dBD95]   M. de Berg and K. Dobrindt. On levels of detail in terrains. In *Proc. 11th Annu. ACM Sympos. Comput. Geom.*, pages C26–C27, 1995.

[dC76]   M. P. do Carmo. *Differential Geometry of Curve and Surfaces*. Prentice-Hall, Englewood Cliffs, 1976.

[DCH88]   R. A. Drebin, L. Carpenter, and P. Hanrahan. Volume rendering. *Computer Graphics*, 22(4):65–74, August 1988.

[DE95]   Delfinado and Edelsbrunner. An incremental algorithm for betti numbers of simplicial complexes on the 3-sphere. *Computer Aided Geometric Design*, 12, 1995.

[Del94]   T. Delmarcelle. *The Visualization of Second-Order Tensor Fields*. PhD thesis, Stanford University, 1994. Ginzton Lab Report 5228.

[DFP85]   L. DeFloriani, B. Falcidieno, and C. Pienovi. Delaunay-based representation of surfaces defined over arbitrarily shaped domains. *Computer Vision, Graphics and Image Processing*, 32:127–140, 1985.

[DH73]   R. P. Duda and P. E. Hart. Pattern classification and scene analysis, 1973.

[DH92]   J. Danskin and P. Hanrahan. Fast algorithms for volume ray tracing. In *Proceedings of 1992 Workshop on Volume Visualization*, pages 91–105, Boston, MA, October 1992.

[Dil81]   J. Dill. An application of color graphics to the display of surface curvature. *Computer Graphics*, 15(3):153–161, 1981.

[DJL92a]   R. DeVore, B. Jawerth, and B. J. Lucier. Image compression through wavelet transform coding. *IEEE Transactions on Information Theory*, 38:719–746, 1992.

[DJL92b]   R. A. DeVore, B. Jawerth, and B. J. Lucier. Surface compression. *Computer Aided Geometric Design*, 9:219–239, 1992.

[DK91]   A. Doi and A. Koide. An efficient method of triangulating equi-valued surfaces by using tetrahedral cells. *IEICE Trans. Commun. Elec. Inf. Syst.*, E-74(1):214–224, 1991.

[Dov95]   D. Dovey. Vector plots for irregular grids. In *Visualization '95*, Atlanta, GA, 1995. IEEE Computer Society Press.

[Dur88]   M. J. Durst. Additional reference to marching cubes. *Computer Graphics*, 22(2):72–73, 1988.

[EDD+95]   M. Eck, T. DeRose, T. Duchamp, H. Hoppe, M. Lounsbery, and W. Stuetzle. Multiresolution analysis of arbitrary meshes. In R. Cook, editor, *SIGGRAPH '95 Conference Proceedings*, Annual Conference Series, pages 173–182. ACM SIGGRAPH, Addison Wesley, August 1995. held in Los Angeles, California, 06-11 August 1995.

[Ede89]   H. Edelsbrunner. An acyclicity theorem in cell complexes in d dimensions. In *Proceedings of the ACM Symposium on Computational Geometry*, pages 145–151. ACM, 1989.

[Ede95]   H. Edelsbrunner. The union of balls and its dual shape. *GEOMETRY: Discrete & Computational Geometry*, 13, 1995.

[Eis76]   L. P. Eisenhart. *An introduction to differential geometry*. Princeton University Press, Princeton, NJ, 1976.

[Far87]   R. Farouki. Graphical methods for surface differential geometry. In R. Martin, editor, *The Mathematics of Surfaces II*, pages 363–386. Oxford University Press, 1987.

[Far88]   G. Farin. *Curves and surfaces for computer aided geometric design*. Academic Press, 1988.

[FFNP84]   L. D. Floriani, B. Falcidieno, G. Nagy, and C. Pienovi. A hierarchical structure for surface approximation. *Computers and Graphics*, 8(2):183–193, 1984.

[FGR85]   G. Frieder, D. Gordon, and R. A. Reynolds. Back-to-front display of voxel-based objects. *IEEE Computer Graphics & Applications*, 5(1):52–60, January 1985.

[FL79]   R. J. Fowler and J. J. Little. Automatic extraction of irregular network digital terrain models. In *Computer Graphics (SIGGRAPH '79 Proceedings)*, volume 13(3), pages 199–207, 1979.

[FLN+90]   T. Foley, D. Lane, G. Nielson, R. Franke, and H. Hagen. Interpolation of scattered data on closed surfaces. *Computer Aided Geometric Design*, 7:303–312, 1990.

[For79]   A. R. Forrest. On the rendering of surfaces. *Computer Graphics*, 13:253–259, 1979.

[For94]   L. Forssell. Visualizing flow over curvilinear grid surfaces using line integral convolution. *Proceedings of IEEE Visualization '94*, pages 240–247, 1994.

[Fru92]   T. Fruhauff. Volume rendering on a multiprocessor architecture with shared memory: A concurrent volume rendering algorithm. In *Proceedings of the Third Eurographics Workshop on Scientific Visualization*, Pisa, Italy, April 1992.

[FS89]   G. Farin and N. Sapidis. Curvature and the fairness of curves and surfaces. *IEEE Computer Graphics & Applications 9*, pages 52–57, 1989.

[FS93]   T. A. Funkhouser and C. H. Sequin. Adaptive display algorithm for interactive frame rates during visualization of complex virtual environments. In *Computer Graphics (SIGGRAPH '93 Proceedings)*, volume 27, pages 247–254, 1993.

[FS94]   A. Finkelstein and D. H. Salesin. Multiresolution curves. In A. Glassner, editor, *Proceedings of SIGGRAPH '94 (Orlando, Florida, July 24–29, 1994)*, Computer Graphics Proceedings, Annual Conference Series, pages 261–268. ACM SIGGRAPH, ACM Press, July 1994. ISBN 0-89791-667-0.

[FvDFH90] J. D. Foley, A. van Dam, S. K. Feiner, and J. F. Hughes. *Computer Graphics: Principles and Practice, 2nd edn.* Addison-Wesley, Reading, MA, 1990.

[FZY84]   E. J. Farrell, R. Zappulla, and W. C. Yang. Color 3d imaging of normal and pathologic intracranial structures. *IEEE Computer Graphics & Applications*, 4(9):5–17, September 1984.

[Gal91]   R. S. Gallagher. Span filtering: An efficient scheme for volume visualization of large finite element models. In G. M. Nielson and L. Rosenblum, editors, *Proceedings of IEEE Visualization '91*, pages 68–75, 1991.

[Gar90]   M. Garrity. Tracing irregular volume data. *Computer Graphic*, 24(5):35–40, November 1990.

[GLF⁺95]   P. R. Ghosh, D. H. Laidlaw, K. W. Fleischer, A. H. Barr, and R. E. Jacobs. Pure phase-encoded MRI and classification of solids. *IEEE Transactions on Medical Imaging*, 14(3):616–620, 1995.

[GLL91]   A. Globus, C. Levit, and T. Lasinski. A tool for visualizing the topology of three-dimensional vector fields. In G. M. Nielson and L. Rosenblum, editors, *Visualization '91 Proceedings*, pages 33–40, 1991. IEEE Computer Society Press.

[GLS⁺97]   G. G. Gornowicz, D. H. Laidlaw, J. W. Shan, D. B. Lang, and P. E. Dimotakis. De-aliasing undersampled volume images for visualization, 1997.

[GR90]   B. Gudmundsson and M. Randen. Incremental generation of projections of CT-volumes. In *Proceedings of the First Conference on Visualization in Biomedical Computing*, pages 27–34, Atlanta, GA, May 1990.

[GR80]   E. Grosse. Approximation and optimization of electron density maps. PhD Thesis, Stanford University, 1980.

[Hai91]   R. Haimes. Techniques for interactive and interrogative scientific volumetric visualization, 1991.

[Ham94]   B. Hamann. A data reduction scheme for triangulated surfaces. In *Computer Aided Geometric Design*, volume 13, pages 197–214. 1994.

[Han90]   P. Hanrahan. Three-pass affine transforms for volume rendering. In *Proceedings SIGGRAPH '90 Conference*, volume 24 of *Computer Graphics*, pages 71–78, November 1990.

[HB94]   C. T. Howie and E. H. Blake. The mesh propagation algorithm for isosurface construction. *Computer Graphics Forum*, 13(3):65–74, 1994. Eurographics '94 Conference issue.

[HB95]   D. Heeger and J. Bergen. Pyramid-based texture analysis and synthesis. In *ACM Computer Graphics Proceedings*, Annual Conference Services, pages 229–238, 1995.

[HC93]   A. J. Hanson and R. A. Cross. Interactive visualization methods for four dimensions. In *Visualization '93*, Boston, MA, 1993. IEEE Computer Society

          Press.

[HCV52]   D. Hilbert and S. Cohn-Vossen. *Geometry and the Imagination*. Chelsea Pub-
          lishing Company, New York, 1952.

[HDD⁺93] H. Hoppe, T. DeRose, T. Duchamp, J. McDonald, and W. Stuetzle. Mesh
          optimization. In J. T. Kajiya, editor, *Computer Graphics (SIGGRAPH '93
          Proceedings)*, volume 27, pages 19–26, 1993.

[Hec86]   P. Heckbert. Survey of texture mapping. *IEEE Computer Graphics & Appli-
          cations*, 6(11):56–67, November 1986.

[HH89]   J. Helman and L. Hesselink. Representation and display of vector field topology
          in fluid flow data sets. *IEEE Computer*, 12(8):27–36, 1989.

[HH90]   J. L. Helman and L. Hesselink. Surface representations of two- and three-
          dimensional fluid flow topology. In *Proceedings of Visualization '90*, pages
          6–13, 1990.

[HH91]   J. L. Hellman and L. Hesselink. Visualizing vector field topology in fluid flows.
          IEEE Computer Graphics & Applications, 11(2):36–46, May 1991.

[HH92]   H. Hagen and S. Hahmann. Generalized focal surfaces: A new method for
          surface interrogation. In *Proceedings Visualization '92*, pages 70–76, Boston,
          MA, 1992.

[HHK⁺95] T. He, L. Hong, A. E. Kaufman, A. Varshney, and S. Wang. Voxel based
          object simplification. In G. M. Nielson and D. Silver, editors, *Visualization '95
          Proceedings*, pages 296–303, 1995.

[HHS⁺92] H. Hagen, S. Hahmann, T. Schreiber, Y. Nakajima, B. Wördenweber, and
          P. Hollemann. Surface interrogation algorithms. *IEEE Computer Graphis &
          Applications*, 12(5):53–60, 1992.

[HHS95]   H. Hagen, S. Hahmann, and T. Schreiber. Visualization of curvature behavior
          of free-form curves and surfaces. *CAD*, 27:545–552, 1995.

[HL92]   J. Hoschek and D. Lasser. Fundamentals of computer aided geometric design,
          1992.

[HM94]   A. J. Hanson and H. Ma. Visualizing flow with quanternion frames. In *Visu-
          alization '94*, Washington, DC, 1994. IEEE Computer Society Press.

[HN82]   R. Hartwig and H. Nowacki. Isolinien und schnitte in coonschen flächen. *Ge-
          ometrisches Modellieren, Informatik Fachberichte der GI*, 65:329–343, 1982. In
          German.

[Hof92]   J. D. Hoffman. Numerical methods for engineers and scientists. McGraw-Hill,
          Inc., New York, 1992.

[Hop96]   H. Hoppe. Progressive meshes. In H. Rushmeier, editor, *SIGGRAPH '96
          Conference Proceedings*, Annual Conference Series, pages 99–108, 1996. Held
          in New Orleans, Louisiana, August 4-9, 1996.

[Hos84]   J. Hoschek. Detecting regions with undesirable curvature. *Computer Aided
          Geometric Design*, 1(2):183–192, 1984.

[Hos85]   J. Hoschek. Smoothing of curves and surfaces. *Computer Aided Geometric
          Design*, 2:97–105, 1985.

[HP93]   A. J. S. Hin and F. Post. Visualization of turbulent flow with particles. In
          Visualization '93, Washington, DC, 1993. IEEE Computer Society Press.

[HU94]   H. M. Hearnshaw and D. J. Unwin, editors. *Visualization in Graphical Infor-
          mation Systems*. John Wiley & Sons, 1994.

[Hul92]   J. P. M. Hultquist. Constructing stream surfaces in steady 3D vector fields.
          In *Visualization '92*, pages 171–178, Los Alamitos, CA, October 1992. IEEE
          Computer Society Press.

[IK95]   T. Itoh and K. Koyamada. Automatic isosurface propagation using an extrema
          graph and sorted boundary cell lists. *IEEE Transactions on Visualization and
          Computer Graphics*, 1(4):319–327, 1995.

[IYK96]   T. Itoh, Y. Yamaguchi, and K. Koyamada. Volume thinning for automatic
          isosurface propagation. In *Proceedings of IEEE Visualization '96*, pages 303–
          310, 1996.

[KCM94]   D. B. Karron, J. Cox, and B. Mishra. New findings from the SpiderWeb algorithm: Toward a digital Morse theory. In *Visualization in Biomedical Computing*, volume 2359, pages 643–657, 1994.

[KCY93]   A. E. Kaufman, D. Cohen, and R. Yagel. Volumetric graphics. *IEEE Computer*, 26(7):51–64, July 1993.

[Ken93]   D. Kenwright. Dual stream function methods for generating three-dimensional streamlines, 1993.

[KH84]   J. T. Kajiya and B. P. V. Herzen. Ray tracing volume densities. *Computer Graphics*, 18(3):165–174, July 1984.

[KH89]   J. T. Kajiya and B. P. V. Herzen. Rendering fur with three dimensional textures. *Computer Graphics*, 23(3):271–280, 1989.

[Kje83]   J. Kjellander. Smoothing of bicubic parametric surfaces. *CAD*, 15:288–293, 1983.

[KK88]   A. E. Kaufmann and R. Klass. Smoothing surfaces using reflection lines for families of splines. *CAD*, 20:312–316, 1988.

[KK93]   P. R. Keller and M. M. Keller. *Visual Cues: Practical Data Visualization*. IEEE Computer Society Press and IEEE Press, 1993.

[Kla80]   R. Klass. Correction of local irregularities using reflection lines. *CAD*, 12:73–77, 1980.

[KM92]   D. Kenwright and G. Mallinson. A 3-D streamline tracking algorithm using dual stream functions. In A. E. Kaufman and G. Nielson, editors, *Proceedings of IEEE Visualization '92 (Boston, Massachusetts, October 19–23, 1992)*, Visualization Conference Series, pages 62–68, 1992.

[Knu73]   D. E. Knuth. *The Art of Computer Programming I: Fundemental Algorithms*, volume 1. Addison Wesley, Reading, Massachusetts, second edition, 1973.

[Kre59]   I. Kreyszing. *Differential Geometry*. University of Toronto Press, 1959.

[Kru90]   W. Krueger. The application of transport theory to visualization of 3D scalar data field. In *Proceedings Visualization '90*, pages 273–280, San Francisco, CA, October 1990.

[KSW96]   Y.-H. Kao, J. A. Sorenson, and S. S. Winkler. MR image segmentation using vector decompsition and probability techniques: A general model and its application to dual-echo images. *Magnetic Resonance in Medicine*, 35:114–125, 1996.

[KV90]   D. Kirk and D. Voorhies. The rendering architecture of the dn1000vs. *Computer Graphics*, 24(4):299–307, 1990.

[KY95]   Y. Kurzion and R. Yagel. Volume deformation using Ray Deflectors. In *The 6th Eurographics Workshop on Rendering*, pages 33–44, Dublin, Ireland, June 1995.

[Lac95]   P. Lacroute. Real-time volume rendering on shared memory multiprocessors using the shear-warp factorization. In *Proceedings 1995 Parallel Rendering Symposium*, pages 15–22, Atlanta, GA, October 1995.

[Lai92]   D. H. Laidlaw. Tissue classification of magnetic resonance volume data, 1992.

[Lai95]   D. H. Laidlaw. Geometric model extraction from magnetic resonance volume data, 1995.

[Lan94]   D. A. Lane. UFAT – A particle tracer for time-dependent flow fields. In *Visualization '93*, pages 257–264, Boston, MA, 1994. IEEE Computer Society Press.

[LBJ97]   D. H. Laidlaw, A. H. Barr, and R. E. Jacobs. Goal-directed brain microimaging. In S. H. Koslow and M. F. Huerta, editors, *Neuroinformatics: An Overview of the Human Brain Project*, volume 1. 1997.

[LC87]   W. E. Lorensen and H. E. Cline. Marching cubes: A high resolution 3D surface construction algorithm. In M. C. Stone, editor, *Computer Graphics (SIGGRAPH '87 Proceedings)*, volume 21, pages 163–169, 1987.

[Lee91]   J. Lee. Comparison of existing methods for building triangular irregular networks. *Int. Journal of Geographical Information Systems*, 5(2):267–285, 1991.

[Lev88a] M. Levoy. Display of surfaces from volume data. *IEEE Computer Graphics & Applications*, 8(5):29–37, May 1988.

[Lev88b]   M. Levoy. Display of surfaces from volume data. *IEEE Computer Graphics and Applications*, 8(3):29 37, 1988.

[Lev90a]   M. Levoy. Efficient ray tracing of volume data. *ACM Transactions on Graphics*, 9(3):245–261, July 1990.

[Lev90b]   M. Levoy. Volume rendering by adaptive refinement. *The Visual Computer*, 6(1):2–7, February 1990.

[Lev92]   M. Levoy. Volume rendering using the Fourier projection-slice theorem. In *Proceedings of Graphics Interface '92*, pages 61–69, 1992.

[Lew84]   J. P. Lewis. Texture synthesis for digital painting. *Computational Graphics*, 18:245–252, July 1984.

[Lew90]   R. R. Lewis. Three-dimensional texturing using lattices. In *Eurographics '90*. Elsevier Science Publishers B.V., 1990.

[LF84]   R. B. Lee and D. A. Fredericks. Intersection of parametric surfaces and a plane. *IEEE Computer Graphics & Applications*, 4(8):48–51, 1984.

[LFB97]   D. H. Laidlaw, K. W. Fleischer, and A. H. Barr. Partial-volume Bayesian classification of material mixtures in MR volume data using voxel histograms, 1997.

[LH91]   D. Laur and P. Hanrahan. Hierarchical splatting: A progressive refinement algorithm for volume rendering. *Computer Graphics*, 25(4):285–288, July 1991.

[LKR⁺96]   P. Lindstrom, D. Koller, W. Ribarsky, L. F. Hodges, N. Faust, and G. A. Turner. Real-time, continuous level of detail rendering of height fields. In H. Rushmeier, editor, *SIGGRAPH '96 Conference Proceedings*, Annual Conference Series, pages 109–118, 1996. Held in New Orleans, Louisiana, August 4-9, 1996.

[LL94]   P. Lacroute and M. Levoy. Fast volume rendering using a shear-warp factorization of the viewing transformation. In *Proceedings SIGGRAPH '94 Conference*, volume 28 of *Computer Graphics*, pages 451–458, Orlando, FL, July 24-29 1994. ACM SIGGRAPH.

[Lor90]   T. J. Loredo. From Laplace to Supernova SN 1987A: Bayesian inference in astrophysics. In P. F. Fougere, editor, *Maximum Entropy and Bayesian Methods*, pages 81–142. Kluwer Academic Publishers, Denmark, 1990.

[Lor95]   W. E. Lorensen. Marching through the visible man. In G. M. Nielson and D. Silver, editors, *Proceedings of IEEE Visualization '95*, pages 368–373, 1995.

[LSJ96]   Y. Livnat, H.-W. Shen, and C. R. Johnson. A near optimal isosurface extraction algorithm for unstructured grids. *IEEE Transactions on Visualization and Computer Graphics*, 2(1):73–84, 1996.

[Luc92]   B. Lucas. A scientific visualization renderer. In *Proceedings of Visualization '92*, pages 227–234, Los Alamitos, CA, 1992. IEEE Computer Society Press.

[LVG80]   S. Lobregt, P. W. Verbeek, and F. C. A. Groen. Three-dimensional skeletonization: Principle and algorithms. *IEEE Transactions on Pattern Analysis and Machine Intelligence*, 2(1):75–77, 1980.

[LY95]   A. Law and R. Yagel. Cellflow: A parallel rendering scheme for distributed memory architectures. In *Proceedings of International Conference on Parallel and Distributed Processing Techniques and Applications (PDPTA '95)*, pages 1–10, November 1995.

[LY96a]   A. Law and R. Yagel. Exploiting spatial, ray, and frame coherency for efficient parallel volume rendering. In *GRAPHICON '96*, Saint-Petersburg, Russia, July 1996.

[LY96b]   A. Law and R. Yagel. Multi-frame thrashless ray casting with advancing rayfront. In *Graphics Interface '96*, pages 71–77, Toronto, Canada, May 1996.

[LY96c]   A. Law and R. Yagel. An optimal ray traversal scheme for visualizing colossal medical volumes. *Visualization in Biomedical Computing*, September 1996.

[LYJ96]   A. Law, R. Yagel, and D. N. Jayasimha. Voxelflow: A parallel volume rendering method for scientific visualization. *ISCA Journal of Computers & Their Applications*, April 1996.

[Mal89]   S. G. Mallat. A theory for multiresolution signal decomposition: The wavelet representation. *IEEE Transactions on Pattern Analysis and Machine Intelligence*, 11(7):674–693, July 1989.

[Mal93]   T. Malzbender. Fourier volume rendering. *ACM Transactions on Graphics*, 12(3):233–250, 1993.

[Mat94]   S. V. Matveyev. Approximating of isosurface in the marching cube: Ambiguity problem. In R. D. Bergeron and A. E. Kaufman, editors, *Proceedings of Visualization '94*, pages 288–292, 1994.

[Max93a]   N. Max. New techniques in 3D scalar and vector field visualization. In S. Y. Shin and T. L. Kunii, editors, *Computer Graphics & Applications*, pages 301–315, Singapore, 1993. World Scientific.

[Max93b]   N. Max. Sorting for polyhedron compositing. In H. Müller and G. Nielson, editors, *In Focus on Scientific Visualization*, pages 259–268. Springer Verlag, Berlin, Germany, 1993.

[Max95]   N. Max. Optical models for direct volume rendering. *IEEE Transactions on Visualization & Computer Graphics*, 1(2):99–108, June 1995.

[MBC93]   N. Max, B. Becker, and R. Crawfis. Flow volumes for interactive vector field visualizations. In *Proceedings, Visualization '93*, pages 19–24, Los Alamitos, CA, 1993. IEEE Computer Society Press.

[McC85]   E. M. McCreight. Priority search trees. *SIAM J. Comput.*, 14:257–276, 1985.

[MCG94]   N. Max, R. Crawfis, and C. Grants. Visualizing 3d velocity fields near contour surfaces. In *Proceedings, Visualization '94*, pages 248–255, Los Alamitos, CA, 1994. IEEE Computer Society Press.

[MCW92]   N. Max, R. Crawfis, and D. Williams. Visualizing wind velocities by advecting cloud texture. *Proceedings of IEEE Visualization '92*, pages 179–184, 1992.

[MCW93]   N. Max, R. Crawfis, and D. William. Visualization for climate modeling. *Computer Graphics & Application*, 13(4):34–40, 1993.

[Mea82]   D. Meagher. Geometric modeling using octree encoding. *Computer Graphics & Image Processing*, 19(2):129–147, June 1982.

[Meh84]   K. Mehlhorn. *Data Structures and Algorithms 3: Multi-dimensional Searching and Computational Geometry*, volume 3 of *EATCS Monographs on Theoretical Computer Science*. Springer-Verlag, Heidelberg, West Germany, 1984.

[Mey94]   D. Meyers. Multiresolution tiling. In *Proceedings of Graphics Interface '94*, pages 25–32, Banff, Alberta, Canada, 1994.

[MHC90]   N. Max, P. Hanrahan, and R. Crawfis. Area and volume coherence for efficient visualization of 3D scalar functions. *Computer Graphics*, 24(5):27–33, 1990.

[Mit87]   D. P. Mitchell. Generating antialiased images at low sampling densities. *Computer Graphics*, 21(4):65–72, 1987.

[MMMY96]   T. Moller, R. Machiraju, K. Mueller, and R. Yagel. Classification and local error estimation of interpolation and derivative filters for volume rendering. In *Proceedings of 1996 Symposium on Volume Visualization*, pages 71–78, 1996.

[MP94]   T. Maekawa and M. Patrikalakis. Interrogation of differential geometry properties for design and manufacture. *Visual Computer*, 10:216–237, 1994.

[MPS92]   C. Montani, R. Perego, and R. Scopingo. Parallel volume visualization on a hypercube architecture. In *Proceedings of 1992 Workshop on Volume Visualization*, pages 9–16, Boston, MA, October 1992.

[MS93]   K.-L. Ma and P. J. Smith. Cloud tracing in convection-diffusion systems. In *Visualization '93*, Washington, DC, 1993. IEEE Computer Society Press.

[MSS94]   C. Montani, R. Scateni, and R. Scopigno. Discretized marching cubes. In R. D. Bergeron and A. E. Kaufman, editors, *Proceedings of IEEE Visualization '94*, pages 281–287, 1994.

[Mul94]   K. Mulmuley. *Computational Geometry: An Introduction Through Randomized Algorithms*. Prentice Hall, Englewood Cliffs, NJ, 1994.

[Mur92]   S. Muraki. Approximation and rendering of volume data using wavelet transforms. In A. E. Kaufman and G. M. Nielson, editors, *Proceedings of Visualization '92 (Boston, Massachusetts, October 19–23, 1992)*, pages 21–28. IEEE Computer Society, IEEE Computer Society Press, October 1992.

[Mur95]   S. Muraki. Multiscale volume representation by a DoG wavelet. *IEEE Transactions on Visualization and Computer Graphics*, 1(2):109–116, June 1995. ISSN 1077-2626.

[MWP96]   T. Maekawa, F.-E. Wolter, and N. Patrikalakis. Umbilics and lines of curvature for shape interrogation. *Computer Aided Geometric Design*, 13:133–161, 1996.

[MYS92]   R. Machiraju, R. Yagel, and L. Schwiebert. Parallel algorithms for volume rendering. Technical Report OSU-CISRC-10/92-TR29, The Ohio State University, Department of Computer and Information Science, October 1992.

[MZ94]   K.-L. Ma and Z. C. Zheng. 3D visualization of unsteady 2D airplane wake vortices. In *Visualization '94 Proceedings*, pages 124–131, Washington, DC, 1994. IEEE Computer Society Press.

[Nac84]   L. R. Nackman. Two-dimensional critical point configuration graphs. *IEEE Trans. Pattern Analysis and Machine Intelligence*, 6(4):442–450, 1984.

[Nat94]   B. K. Natarajan. On generating topologically consistent isosurfaces from uniform samples. *The Visual Computer*, 11(1):52–62, 1994.

[Nea95]   H. Nishimura and et al. Object modelling by distribution function and a method of imaging generation. In *Electronics Communication Conference*, 1995.

[NFMD90]   D. R. Ney, E. K. Fishman, D. Magid, and R. A. Drebin. Volumetric rendering of computed tomography data: Principles and techniques. *IEEE Computer Graphics and Applications*, 10(2):24–32, March 1990.

[NH91]   G. M. Nielson and B. Hamann. The asymptotic decider: Resolving the ambiguity of marching cubes. In G. M. Nielson and L. Rosenblum, editors, *Visualization '91 Proceedings*, pages 83–91, 1991.

[NHM97]   G. M. Nielson, H. Hagen, and H. Muller, editors. *Scientific Visualization*. IEEE Computer Society, 1997.

[NL92]   J. Neih and M. Levoy. Volume rendering on scalable shared memory architecture. In *Proceedings of 1992 Workshop on Volume Visualization*, pages 17–24, Boston, MA, October 1992.

[OWY83]   A. V. Oppenheim, A. S. Willsky, and I. T. Young. Signals and systems, 1983.

[PD84]   T. Porter and T. Duff. Compositing digital images. *Computer Graphics*, 18(3):253–359, July 1984.

[PDDT94]   E. Puppo, L. Davis, D. DeMenthon, and Y. Teng. Parallel terrain triangulation. *Int. Journal of Geographical Information Systems*, 8(2):105–128, 1994.

[Pea88]   W. H. Press et al. Numerical recipes in c. Cambridge Press, Cambridge, MA, 1988.

[Per85]   K. Perlin. An image synthesizer. *Computer Graphics (SIGGRAPH '85 Proceedings)*, 19(3):287–296, July 1985.

[Pet84]   C. S. Petersen. Adaptive contouring of three-dimensional surfaces. *Computer Aided Graphic Design*, 1:61–74, 1984.

[Poe84]   T. Poeschl. Detecting surface irregularities using isophotes. *Computer Aided Graphic Design*, 1:163–168, 1984.

[Por94]   I. Porteous. *Geometric Differentiation*. Cambridge University Press, 1994.

[Pot89]   H. Pottmann. Visualizing curvature discontinuities of free-form surfaces. In *Proc. Eurographics '89*, pages 529–536, 1989.

[Pup96]   E. Puppo. Variable resolution terrain surfaces. In F. Fiala, E. Kranakis, and J.-R. Sack, editors, *Canadian Conference on Computational Geometry*, pages 202–210, 1996.

[PW94]   H.-G. Pagendarm and B. Walter. Feature detection from vector quantities in a numerically simulated hypersonic flow field in combination with experimental flow visualization. In *Visualization'94*. IEEE Computer Society Press, 1994.

[RB85]   W. T. Reeves and R. Blau. Approximate and probabilistic algorithms for shading and rendering structured particle systems. *Computer Graphics*, 19(3):313–322, July 1985.

[RB93]   J. Rossignac and P. Borrel. Multi-resolution 3D approximations for rendering complex scenes. In *IFIP TC 5.WG 5.10 II Conference on Geometric Modeling in Computer Graphics*, 1993. IBM Research Report RC 17697, Yorktown

Heights, NY 10598.

[Ree83]   W. T. Reeves. Particle systems – a technique for modeling a class of fuzzy objects. *ACM Transactions on Graphics*, 2(2):91–108, April 1983.

[REE+94]   L. Rosenblum, R. A. Earnshaw, J. Encarnacao, H. Hagen, A. Kaufman, S. Klimenko, G. Nielson, F. Post, and D. Thalmann, editors. *Scientific Visualization: Advances and Challenges.* Academic Press, 1994.

[RGC87]   R. A. Reynolds, D. Gordon, and L. S. Chen. A dynamic screen technique for shaded graphic display of slice-represented objects. *Computer Vision, Graphics & Image Processing*, 38(3):275–298, June 1987.

[RR96]   R. Ronfard and J. Rossignac. Full-range approximation of triangulated polyhedra. In *Eurographics '96*, volume 15. 1996.

[Sab88]   P. Sabella. A rendering algorithm for visualizing 3D scalar fields. *Computer Graphics*, 22(4):51–58, August 1988.

[SBM94]   C. Stein, B. Becker, and N. Max. Sorting and hardware assisted rendering for volume visualization. In *Proceedings 1994 Symposium on Volume Visualization*, pages 83–89. ACM Press, 1994.

[Sch83]   D. Schweitzer. Artificial texturing: An aid to surface visualization. *Computer Graphics*, 17(3):23–29, 1983.

[SCK+93]   L. Sobierajski, D. Cohen, A. E. Kaufman, R. Yagel, and D. Acker. A fast display method for volumetric data. *The Visual Computer*, 10(2):116–124, 1993.

[SDS96]   E. J. Stollnitz, T. D. DeRose, and D. H. Salesin. Wavelets for computer graphics: Theory and applications, 1996.

[SG93]   P. Santago and H. D. Gage. Quantification of MR brain images by mixture density and partial volume modeling. *IEEE Transactions on Medical Imaging*, 12(3):566–574, 1993.

[SH95]   D. Stalling and H.-C. Hege. Fast and resolution independent line integral convolution. In *SIGGRAPH '95 Conference Proceedings*, Annual Conference Series, pages 249–256, 1995.

[SHLJ96]   H.-W. Shen, C. D. Hansen, Y. Livnat, and C. R. Johnson. Isosurfacing in span space with utmost efficiency. In *Visualization '96 Proceedings*, pages 287–294, 1996.

[Sho79]   R. Shoup. Color table animation. *Computer Graphics*, 13(2):8–13, August 1979.

[Sim90]   K. Sims. Particle animation and rendering using data parallel computation. *Computer Graphics*, 24(4):405–413, 1990.

[SJ95]   H.-W. Shen and C. R. Johnson. Sweeping simplices: A fast iso-surface extraction algorithm for unstructured grids. In G. M. Nielson and D. Silver, editors, *Proceedings of IEEE Visualization '95*, pages 143–150, 1995.

[SK90]   D. Speray and S. Kennon. Volume probes: Interactive data exploration on arbitrary grids. *Computer Graphics (San Diego Workshop on Volume Visualization)*, 24(5):5–12, November 1990.

[SMK95]   C. Silva, J. Mitchell, and A. E. Kaufman. Automatic generation of triangular irregular networks using greedy cuts. In G. M. Nielson and D. Silver, editors, *Visualization '95 Proceedings*, pages 201–208, 1995.

[SMW98]   C. Silva, J. Mitchell, and Williams. An exact interactive time visibility ordering algorithm for polyhedrol cell complexes. In *Proceedings, 1998 Symposium on Volume Visualization* 1998. IEEE Computer Society Press.

[SR85]   S. G. Scatterfield and D. F. Rogers. Contour lines from a B-spline surface. *IEEE Computer Graphics & Applications*, 5(4):71–75, 1985.

[Sri81]   S. N. Srihari. Representation of three-dimensional digital images. *Computing Surveys*, 13(4):399–424, 1981.

[SS91]   P. Schroeder and J. B. Salem. Fast rotation of volume data on data parallel architecture. In *Proceedings of Visualization '91*, pages 50–57, San Diego, CA, October 1991.

[SS92]   P. Schroeder and G. Stoll. Data parallel volume rendering as line drawing. In *Proceedings of 1992 Workshop on Volume Visualization*, pages 25–31, Boston,

MA, October 1992.

[SSO96]   M. Sanner, J.-C. Spehner, and A. Olson. Reduced surface: an efficient way to compute molecular surfaces. *Biopolymers*, 38(3):305–320, 1996.

[SSW86]   D. S. Schlusselberg, K. Smith, and D. J. Woodward. Three-dimensional display of medical image volumes. In *Proceedings of NCGA '86 Conference, III*, pages 114–123, May 1986.

[ST90]   P. Shirley and A. Tuchman. A polygonal approximation to direct scalar volume rendering. *Computer Graphics*, 24(5):63–70, November 1990.

[Str86]   G. Strang. *Introduction to Applied Mathematics*, chapter 8.2 : The simplex method and Karmarkar's method, pages 673–689. Wellesley–Cambridge–Press, Cambridge, MA, USA, 1986.

[SVL91]   W. J. Schroeder, C. R. Volpe, and W. E. Lorenson. The stream polygon: A technique for 3D vector field visualization. In *Visualization '91*, San Diego, CA, October 1991. IEEE Computer Society Press.

[SZL92]   W. J. Schroeder, J. A. Zarge, and W. E. Lorensen. Decimation of triangle meshes. In E. E. Catmull, editor, *Computer Graphics (SIGGRAPH '92 Proceedings)*, volume 26(2), pages 65–70, 1992.

[TL93]   T. Totsuka and M. Levoy. Frequency domain volume rendering. In J. T. Kajiya, editor, *Computer Graphics (SIGGRAPH '93 Proceedings)*, volume 27, pages 271–278, August 1993.

[Tsa93]   V. J. D. Tsai. Delaunay triangulations in TIN creation: an overview and a linear-time algorithm. *Int. Journal of Geographical Information Systems*, 7(6):501–524, 1993.

[TT84]   H. K. Tuy and L. T. Tuy. Direct 2-d display of 3-d objects. *IEEE Computer Graphics & Applications*, 4(10):29–33, November 1984.

[Tur92]   G. Turk. Re-tiling polygonal surfaces. In E. E. Catmull, editor, *Computer Graphics (SIGGRAPH '92 Proceedings)*, volume 26(2), pages 55–64, 1992.

[UK88]   C. Upson and M. Keeler. V-BUFFER: Visible volume rendering. *Computer Graphics*, 22(4):59–64, August 1988.

[USM95]   S. K. Ueng, K. Sikorski, and K.-L. Ma. Algorithms for visualizing fluid motion in fast algorithms for visualizing fluid motion in steady flown on unstructured grids. In *Visualization'95*, Atlanta, GA, 1995. IEEE Computer Society Press.

[van93]   J. J. van Wijk. Implicit stream surfaces. In *Proceedings of IEEE Visualization '93*, pages 245–252, October 1993.

[VBJ+85]   M. W. Vannier, R. L. Butterfield, D. Jordan, W. A. Murphy, R. G. Levitt, and M. Gado. Multispectral analysis of magnetic resonance images. *Radiology*, 154:221–224, 1985.

[VFR92]   G. Vezina, P. Fletcher, and P. K. Robertson. Volume rendering on the MasPar MP-1. In *Proceedings of 1992 Workshop on Volume Visualization*, pages 3–8, Boston, MA, October 1992.

[vGW93]   A. van Gelder and J. Wilhelms. Rapid exploration of curvilinear grids using direct volume rendering (extended abstract). In *Proceedings of Visualization '92*, pages 70–77, Los Alamitos, CA, 1993. IEEE Computer Society Press.

[vGW94]   A. van Gelder and J. Wilhelms. Topological considerations in isosurface generation. *ACM Transactions on Graphics*, 13(4):337–375, 1994.

[vK96]   M. van Kreveld. Efficient methods for isoline extraction from a digital elevation model based on triangulated irregular networks. *International Journal of Geographical Information Systems*, 10:523–540, 1996. Also appeared as Technical Report UU-CS-1994-21, University of Utrecht, the Netherlands.

[VSR88]   M. W. Vannier, C. M. Speidel, and D. L. Rickman. Magnetic resonance imaging multispectral tissue classification. In *Proc. Neural Information Processing Systems (NIPS)*, 1988.

[vvB+97]   M. van Kreveld, R. van Oostrum, C. L. Bajaj, V. Pascucci, and D. R. Schikore. Contour trees and small seed sets for isosurface traversal. In *13th ACM Symposium on Computational Geometry*, pages 212–220, 1997.

[vW91]   J. J. van Wijk. Spot noise: Texture synthesis for data visualization. *Computer*

Graphics, 25(4):309–318, July 1991.

[vW92]   J. J. van Wijk. Rendering surface-particles. In *Visualization '92 Proceedings*, pages 54–61, Los Alamitos, CA, 1992. IEEE Computer Society Press.

[vW93a]   J. J. van Wijk. Flow visualization with surface particles. *IEEE Computer Graphics & Applications*, 13(4):18–24, July 1993.

[vW93b]   J. J. van Wijk. Implicit stream surfaces. In *Visualization '93*, Los Alamitos, CA, October 1993. IEEE Computer Society Press.

[vWHVP91]   T. van Walsum, A. J. S. Hin, J. Versloot, and F. H. Post. Efficient hybrid rendering of volume data and polygons. In *Second Eurographics Workshop on Visualization in Scientific Computing*, Delft, Netherlands, April 1991.

[WAAR⁺88]   J. P. Windham, M. A. Abd-Allah, D. A. Reimann, J. W. Froelich, and A. M. Haggar. Eigenimage filtering in MR imaging. *Journal of Computer Assisted Tomography*, 12(1):1–9, 1988.

[Wat92]   D. F. Watson. *Contouring*. Pergamon, 1992.

[WCW88]   Z. Wu, H.-W. Chung, and F. W. Wehrli. A bayesian approach to subvoxel tissue classification in NMR microscopic images of trabecular bone. *Journal of Computer Assisted Tomography*, 12(1):1–9, 1988.

[Wes89]   L. Westover. Interactive volume rendering. In *Proceedings of the Chapel Hill Workshop on Volume Visualization*, pages 9–16, Chapel Hill, NC, May 1989. ACM Press.

[Wes90]   L. Westover. Footprint evaluation for volume rendering. *Computer Graphics*, 24(4):367–376, August 1990.

[WG90]   J. Wilhelms and A. V. Gelder. Octrees for faster isosurface generation extended abstract. *Computer Graphics (San Diego Workshop on Volume Visualization)*, 24(5):57–62, 1990.

[Wil78]   L. Williams. Pyramidal parametric. *Computer Graphics*, 12(4):270–274, August 1978.

[Wil92]   P. Williams. Visibility ordering meshed polyhedra. *ACM Transactions on Graphics*, 11(2):103–126, April 1992.

[WJ92]   J. M. Ware and C. B. Jones. A multiresolution topographic surface database. *Int. Journal of Geographical Information Systems*, 6(6):479–496, 1992.

[WM92]   P. Williams and N. Max. A volume density optical model. In *Proceedings 1992 Workshop on Volume Visualization*, pages 61–68, Boston, MA, October 1992. ACM.

[WMS98]   P. Williams, N. Max, and C. Stein. A high accuracy volume renderer for unstructured data. *IEEE Transactions on Visualization and Computer Graphics*, 4(1), 1998.

[WMW86]   G. Wyvill, C. McPheeters, and B. Wyvill. Data structure for soft objects. *The Visual Computer*, 2:227–234, 1986.

[Wol90]   G. Wolberg. *Digital Image Warping*. IEEE Computer Society Press, 10662 Los Vaqueros Circle, Los Alamitos, CA, 1990. IEEE Computer Society Press Monograph.

[WS93]   C. M. Wittenbrink and A. K. Somani. 2D and 3D optimal image warping. In *Proceedings of Seventh International Parallel Processing Symposium*, pages 197–208, Newport Beach, CA, April 1993.

[WV94]   J. Wilhelms and A. Van Gelder. Multi-dimensional trees for controlled volume rendering and compression. In A. Kaufman and W. Krueger, editors, *1994 Symposium on Volume Visualization*, pages 27–34. ACM SIGGRAPH, October 1994.

[WvG90]   J. Wilhelms and A. van Gelder. Topological considerations in isosurface generation. In *Computer Graphics (San Diego Workshop on Volume Visualization)*, pages 79–86, 1990. Published as *Computer Graphics (San Diego Workshop on Volume Visualization)*, volume 24, number 5.

[WvG92]   J. Wilhelms and A. van Gelder. Octrees for faster isosurface generation. *ACM Transactions on Graphics*, 11(3):201–227, 1992.

[Yag91]   R. Yagel. *Efficient methods for volume graphics*. PhD thesis, SUNY at Stony

Brook, Department of Computer Science, December 1991.

[Yag92]   R. Yagel. High quality template-based volume viewing. Technical Report OSU-CISRC-10/92-TR28, The Ohio State University, Department of Computer and Information Science, October 1992.

[Yan94]   W.-J. Yang. Computer-assisted flow visualization. CRC Press, Boca Raton, FL, 1994.

[YCK92]   R. Yagel, D. Cohen, and A. E. Kaufman. Discrete ray tracing. *IEEE Computer Graphics & Applications*, 12(5):19–28, September 1992.

[YESK95]   R. Yagel, D. S. Ebert, J. Scott, and Y. Kurzion. Grouping volume renderers for enhanced visualization in computational fluid dynamics. *IEEE Transactions on Visualization & Computer Graphics*, 1(2):117–132, July 1995.

[YK92]   R. Yagel and A. E. Kaufman. Template-based volume viewing. *Computer Graphics Forum*, 11(3):153–157, September 1992.

[YM95]   R. Yagel and R. Machiraju. Data parallel volume rendering algorithms. *The Visual Computer*, 11(6):319–338, 1995.

[YNF⁺92]   T. Yoo, S. Neumann, U. Fuchs, H. Pizer, S. M. Cullip, J. T. Rhoades, and R. Whitaker. Direct visualization of volume data. *Computer Graphics & Applications*, 12(4):63–71, July 1992.

[YS93]   R. Yagel and Z. Shi. Accelerating volume animation by space-leaping. In *Proceedings of Visualization '93*, pages 62–69, San Jose, CA, October 1993.

[YSW⁺96]   R. Yagel, D. Stredney, G. J. Wiet, P. Schmalbrock, L. Rosenberg, D. Sessanna, Y. Kurzion, and S. King. Multisensory platform for surgical simulation. In *IEEE Virtual Reality Annual International Symposium 1996 – VRAIS'96*, pages 72–78, Santa Clara, CA, March 1996.

[ZCK97]   Y. Zhou, B. Chen, and A. Kaufman. Multiresolution tetrahedral framework for visualizing volume data. In *Proceedings of IEEE Visualization '97*, pages 135–142, October 1997.

[ZCT95]   Y. Zhou, W. Chen, and Z. Tang. An elaborate ambiguity detection method for constructing isosurfaces within tetrahedral meshes. *Computers and Graphics*, 19(3):355–364, 1995.

[ZKV92]   K. Zuiderveld, A. H. J. Koning, and M. A. Viergever. Acceleration of ray casting using 3D distance transforms. In *Proceedings of Visualization in Biomedical Computing*, pages 324–335, October 1992.

[ZSS97]   D. Zorin, P. Schröder, and W. Sweldens. Interactive multiresolution mesh editing. In T. Whitted, editor, *SIGGRAPH 97 Conference Proceedings*, Annual Conference Series, pages 259–268. ACM SIGGRAPH, Addison Wesley, August 1997.